MW01269041

Why Be a Christian?

The Sermons of
Howard P. Giddens

Howard Peterson Giddens

Why Be a Christian?

The Sermons of
Howard P. Giddens

compiled and edited by
Michael L. Ruffin

To Fred + Ann, with
gratitude.

Michael L. Ruffin
7/11/07

MERCER
UNIVERSITY PRESS

MUP/H741

The paper used in this publication meets the minimum requirements
of American National Standard for Information Sciences—
Permanence of Paper for Printed Library Materials,
ANSI Z39.48-1984.

Library of Congress Cataloging-in-Publication Data

Giddens, Howard P.
    Why be a Christian? : the sermons of Howard P. Giddens / compiled
and edited by Michael L. Ruffin. – 1st ed.
        p.   cm.
    ISBN-13: 978-0-88146-081-0 (hardcover : alk. paper)
    ISBN-10: 0-88146-081-8 (hardcover : alk. paper)
    1. Baptists–Sermons. 2. Sermons, American 20th century. I. Ruffin,
Michael Lee, 1958–   II. Title.
BX6333.G485W49 2007
252'.061--dc22

                                                        2007012032

Contents

Foreword

To hold a collection of sermons by Dr. Howard P. Giddens is to hold precious renderings, put to paper, of what was born in his heart, believed in his soul, shared in his wise counsel, and lived out in his life. Though he never had children of his own, Dr. Giddens has been a Father in the Faith to so many of us. He never sought that designation nor did he accept it without reservation. Dr. Giddens earned this place in so many of our lives simply by being interested, available, and always engaged in the conversations that filled and defined our lives.

One of my earliest memories of Mercer University is of my dad, Charles Elder, taking me to Dr. Giddens's Adams Street residence on the Mercer campus to see a man of whom he said, "I just want you to get to know him."

I had long heard of Dr. Giddens and had met him on occasion, but on that afternoon as we sat in the living room of that cottage, I felt that I was in the presence of greatness. It was a little intimidating to be sure, but in moments I learned that Dr. Giddens was interested in *me*. He talked to *me*. He was interested in what was bringing *me* to Mercer.

He told a story or two and soon he was more than someone Dad wanted me to get to know; he was a person whom I knew and had begun to love. Dr. Giddens has always had that kind of effect upon people. That Adams Street home was a madhouse of activity as students, friends, former parishioners, and people from every walk of life came to chat with Dr. Giddens. There was always room for one more friend, one more question, one more conversation, one more bit of wise counsel, a few more minutes for him to listen.

When you read the sermons in this book you will find a curious blend of scholarship, social awareness, humor, and humanity filtered through an uncompromising faith and love for the Lord and for people. This is the same way he related to us as students. He connected with his classes in a way seen only in rare instances. He knew his students as completely as one could and constantly made opportunities to get to know them better.

His office was at the end of the hall, at the top of the stairs. I do not remember the door ever being completely shut. He was interruptible while never being interrupted. He and Mrs. Giddens opened their home to students even as they had to their parishioners during their days in the pastorate. But I especially remember the dimly lit hall of Knight Hall and the brightness of the light from his office. So many entered dim with conflicted feelings or questions and left with the light of hope. That office was filled with the light of wisdom, acceptance, and care, often offered with humor that did not allow us to be self-absorbed or hopeless. No wonder everyone wanted to have a course with Dr. Giddens and most claimed him as a "best friend."

A number of years ago, several of us were working on a project that would recognize the contribution that Dr. Giddens has made to our lives. I wrote about the open door and light from the office at the top of the stairs. We were determined to do something that would always keep this light on and the door open for generations that might not have a chance to sit and talk with this wonderful teacher. I think that Dr. Ruffin has found a way in the publishing of this book. Each of Dr. Giddens's students could add memories that would be as unique as the individual relationship and as common as Dr. Giddens's commitment to people and to the Lord.

Several years ago, I wrote "Dr. G" and told him how much his life and ministry had meant in my life. I told him that his always being there, always believing in me, and always influencing and encouraging my life was a key to the happiness and fulfillment that I have today. I told him that anything I ever did would bear the mark of his touch for as long as I lived. I mailed the letter with great satisfaction realizing how seldom we say what we should before it is too late. After I mailed it, I had this image of Dr. Giddens receiving it, reading it, and then putting it in a special place where he would keep the blessing that I offered. In my imagination, this place was stuffed with thousands of other such notes that told of how he has been to others what he has been to me. Every one of these lives has the potential to keep the door cracked and the light shining through for others with whom we may share the wisdom and care that we experienced at the feet of this pastor, teacher, and friend.

Indeed, I thank my God upon every remembrance of Dr. Giddens. These sermons help me to relive the words and spirit of this man of God.

James C. Elder, Jr.
Pastor, First Baptist Church, Columbus, Georgia

Editor's Preface

This book is a labor of love. I have been blessed in my life to be able to love two men as father. One was my father, Champ Lee Ruffin, who brought me into this world and who raised me through my childhood, youth, and college years. He died eleven months after I graduated from Mercer University. The other was my father in the ministry and my father in every way that matters ever since my own father died, Dr. Howard Peterson Giddens. My father was in my life for twenty-one years. Dr. Giddens has been part of my life for more than thirty years. I am honored to have been loved by both of them. I am honored to have had the privilege to love both of them. Perhaps one day I will write a book about my father, a good and fascinating man in his own right. Today I am glad to have been able to put together a book made up of the words of my second father.

The day I met Dr. Giddens—even though we developed a father-son relationship, he has always been "Dr. Giddens" to me—is one of the most significant days of my life. It was the summer of 1975. I was set to enter Mercer University that fall as a member of the freshman class. My admissions counselor asked me what major I was considering and whether I had any thoughts as to my career. "I'm going to be a minister," I answered, "so I'll probably major in Christianity."

"There's someone I want you to meet," he said. He picked up the phone and spoke with someone for a moment. Hanging up, he said, "Good, he's there. Let's go." We walked across the campus to Knight Hall and went up to the office at the top of the stairs. And there I met Dr. Giddens. I probably spent an hour with him that first day. His interest and care were obvious and genuine. He offered to be my academic advisor. He became my friend, mentor, guide, teacher, and, as I have already said, my father.

I had come to Mercer out of a background not unlike that of many students in those days and I guess in all days. My home was small and rural, my family was good and faithful, and my church was sincere and simple. I knew little of educated ministry, nothing of biblical scholarship, and almost nothing of the ways of the wide, wide world. I was frankly scared. During the fall quarter of my freshman year I took Dr. Giddens's course "Introduction to the Old Testament." I was amazed by the experience. We read and he talked about critical approaches to the Bible, about the findings of modern scholarship, and about angles and viewpoints on the biblical stories that I had never seen before. It could have been tough to deal with. Maybe it was tough to deal with. The academic expectations of the course were certainly tough! The thing was, though, that Dr. Giddens brought such integrity to the entire enterprise. He clearly loved the Lord. He clearly loved the church. He clearly loved the Bible. He clearly loved learning. And he clearly loved us, his students. He was there to do good. He was there to do good by us. He was there to do good by the Bible. He modeled Christian, pastoral scholarship. It was a wonderful experience.

It was such a wonderful experience that I took a total of five courses with him at Mercer. Back then eight courses constituted a major, so my major in Christianity was practically a major in Dr. Giddens. It is a major that has served me well, because the Dr. Giddens type of Christianity is what I have always tried to live out in my own life. I think that the same has been true of vast numbers of his parishioners and students. I have to put it that way, because Dr. Giddens is both a pastor and a teacher. He spent thirty years serving as the pastor of Baptist churches before he became a professor at Mercer. His words and his influence flowed from both pulpit and lectern. His wisdom was shared in both pastor's study and teacher's office. His grace was communicated in both church and school. He has touched an untold number of lives. He has loved and been loved by an unfathomable multitude of people. I hope that this collection of his sermons will allow his influence, his wisdom, his grace, and his love to continue to touch people for decades to come, for his legacy is one that deserves to be kept alive.

The sermons in this collection were prepared and preached by Dr. Giddens between the 1930s and the 1960s. The earliest ones were written while he was pastor of the New Castle (Kentucky) Baptist Church, during his years as a seminary student. The latest ones were written while he was pastor of the First Baptist Church of Athens, Georgia, his last pastorate before going to Mercer to teach. He filed each sermon in an individual envelope on which he wrote the title of the sermon, the scripture text, and the places at which and the dates on which he preached it. Many of these sermons were pulled from envelopes on which a long list of places and dates is written. I like to think of those as his greatest hits.

The sermons are written and were preached in a style that can now be regarded as classical. They reverberate with sacredness and dignity even as they sparkle with wit and warmth. They reveal the heart of a man who believed in the Savior he was proclaiming and the Book that he was preaching. I have entitled the collection *Why Be a Christian?*, a title that is taken from one of the sermons, because that is a theme that emerges from sermon after sermon after sermon. Dr. Giddens is a joyful Christian who wants everyone to know the kind of joy he knows. After reading his sermons, after weighing his evidence and getting a sense of his heart, the question one would have to ask oneself is, "Why not be a Christian?"

Dr. Giddens's sermons were of course prepared for delivery from the pulpit, not for publication. So his quotations of a whole range of literature and documents were acknowledged only by very general references to an author or text. He was, like all effective preachers, inspired and instructed by good writers and by other effective preachers. The thoughts and words of those other wordsmiths surely echo within Dr. Giddens's words. So that proper credit may be given to previously published sources, an attempt has been made to document at least his major references. References that could not be identified are placed in bracketed footnotes. Without access to Dr. Giddens's original notes, it was not possible to determine a source for every reference. Please advise the publisher if you recognize any undocumented copyrighted source, and subsequent editions will include that reference. We apologize for any oversight.

I am grateful to Dr. Giddens' wife, Gladys Holder Giddens, for making his sermons available to me. She allowed me to take all of his sermons that we could find so that I could work on this collection. In so doing she trusted me with a great treasure. I am grateful to Mrs. Giddens for her support and encouragement of this project. I am also grateful to her for her support and encouragement in many other ways over the years. She has been mother to me just as surely as Dr. Giddens has been father. One cannot think of Dr. Giddens without also thinking of Mrs. Giddens. They have been a tremendous team through whom the kingdom of God has been enriched and by whom countless people have been blessed.

I am also grateful to Dr. Marc Jolley of the Mercer University Press for his support of this project. He also knows and appreciates Dr. Giddens, who has served on the Mercer University Press board of directors since the inception of the Press. It is fitting that this collection be published by the Press that Dr. Giddens loved and served and by the Press that is associated with the University that was Dr. Giddens's learning and teaching home for so many years.

Dr. Giddens's sermons had to be retyped so that they could be arranged and edited and the project would have stretched on much longer than it did had I not had significant help. I am grateful to Wyanne Moseley, administrative assistant at The Hill Baptist Church, and to Rev. Fred Gunter, associate pastor emeritus at The Hill Baptist Church and fellow Mercer alumnus, for their invaluable assistance in typing.

Finally, I am grateful to my wife, Debra Johnson Ruffin, who typed many of these sermons and who has been a constant source of encouragement in this and in every other project I have ever attempted. This has also been a labor of love for her. She too is a Mercer graduate. She too took Dr. Giddens's "Old Testament Introduction" in the fall quarter of her freshman year at Mercer. She too fell in love with him. He has been father and mentor to her also. I'm glad that we have been able to share in this project as we have shared in everything else for three decades now.

Michael L. Ruffin

Acknowledgments

Publication of this volume is made possible in part by the contributions of the following persons–in honor of Dr. Giddens, and by the endowment support of Tom Watson Brown† and the Watson-Brown Foundation.

A. T. and Elna Bragdon
Nashville, Georgia

Jimmy and Roxann Elder
Columbus, Georgia

Margaret Ann McConnell
Alpharetta, Georgia

Patsy Adams
Middleburg, Florida

Robert W. Gaskins
Nashville, Georgia

Doug Gaskins
Nashville, Georgia

Mr. and Mrs. Joseph K. Leaphart
Greenville, South Carolina

Billy and Sandra Lynn
Augusta, Georgia

Jimmy Mills
Augusta, Georgia

Dane and Danita Perkins
Nashville, Georgia

John B. Prince III
Tifton, Georgia

MERCER
UNIVERSITY PRESS

Endowed by
TOM WATSON BROWN
and
THE WATSON-BROWN FOUNDATION, INC.

Biographical Introduction

Howard Peterson Giddens was born on 28 November 1910, in Berrien County, Georgia to Albert Holmes Giddens and Minnie Jane Gaskins Giddens. He was the youngest of five children. Following his graduation from Nashville, Georgia High School, he attended Norman College in Norman Park, Georgia for one year. He then entered Mercer University in the fall of 1928. The events of the Great Depression forced him to leave Mercer and go home to Nashville to work for a few years. He returned to Mercer and earned a B.A. in History in 1934 and an M.A. in History and Economics in 1935. He thereby shared in a family tradition of being educated at Georgia Baptist colleges. His brother Holmes also graduated from Mercer and his sisters Christy, Mildred, and Ruth all graduated from Tift College. He was ordained to the ministry on 31 August 1935 by the First Baptist Church of Nashville, Georgia.

He earned two degrees from the Southern Baptist Theological Seminary in Louisville, Kentucky, the Th.M. in 1938 and the Th.D. in 1946. His doctoral dissertation, written under the supervision of Dr. Harold Tribble, was entitled "The Development of Hebrew Monotheism in the Old Testament as Exhibited in the Names Used." During his seminary years, he served as pastor of the New Castle Baptist Church in New Castle, Kentucky (1937–1942).

He married Gladys May Holder, who was also a Mercer graduate, in 1940 at the Little Church on the Corner in New York City. Her father, Dr. Francis Jerome Holder, had served as a Mathematics professor at Mercer until his death in 1931. The wedding was a double wedding with Mrs. Giddens's sister Lois and her groom Richard Hagan.

Dr. Giddens served as pastor of three Baptist churches in Georgia: First Baptist Church of West Point (1942–1947), First Baptist Church of Bainbridge (1947–1949), and First Baptist Church of Athens (1949–1967). Mercer University honored him with the Doctor of Divinity degree in 1955.

A true denominational statesman, Dr. Giddens served the Georgia Baptist Convention in many ways. He served as a member of the boards of trustees of Mercer University (1944–1949), Norman College (1948), Truett-McConnell College (1961–1965), and Baptist Village (1958–1962). He was a member of the executive committee (1953–1958) and chairman of that committee (1954–1958). He preached the convention's annual sermon in 1953. He was president of the convention from 1958 to 1960.

Dr. Giddens also served the Southern Baptist Convention in many roles, including service on the Foreign Mission Board (1955–1961), the executive committee (1961–1967; secretary, 1965–1967), and the committee on boards (three times).

Dr. Giddens joined the faculty of the Department of Christianity at Mercer University in 1967. He was Curry Professor of Christianity from 1967 to 1984. In addition to survey courses in Old Testament and New Testament, he taught upper level Old Testament courses and courses in the practice of ministry. He was the first recipient of the Zeta Omega Zeta Chapter, Lambda Chi Alpha "Outstanding Faculty Member" award which they named "The Howard P. Giddens Award" (1975). The *Baptist Program* listed him as one of the outstanding dedicated teachers in Baptist Colleges (1977).

He assisted in reorganizing the Baptist Student Union at Mercer and throughout his career there he continued to serve as BSU advisor, a role in which Mrs. Giddens served as full partner. He served as assistant to the president for Denominational Relations from 1982 to 1984. He retired from the University in 1984. During his years at Mercer, Dr. Giddens served numerous churches as interim pastor, supply preacher, and Bible study leader.

Dr. Giddens is Emeritus Professor of Christianity at Mercer University. He is a member and deacon of the First Baptist Church of Christ of Macon, Georgia. He is a member of the Mercer Orange Coat Club and the Rotary Club.

Part 1

Jesus Christ

The Formidableness of Jesus

Every one that falleth on that stone shall be broken to pieces; but
on whomsoever it shall fall, it will scatter him as dust.

(Luke 20:18 ASV)

It is difficult to associate the idea of formidableness with our conception of Jesus. Webster defines "formidable" this way: "Exciting fear or dread; adapted to excite fear or deter from approach, encounter, or undertaking; alarming." The synonyms for "formidable" are words like these: "dreadful, fearful, menacing, threatening."

Great Britain has a battleship called the *Formidable*. The word fits a battleship, for a battleship is a fearful, terrible, frightening thing. But it seems a ridiculous word to apply to Jesus. We think of him as the "gentle Jesus, meek and mild," as the children's hymn puts it. He spoke of himself as being "meek and lowly in heart." He dealt tenderly with the sinful and erring. He never broke a bruised reed or quenched a flickering wick. As we imagine this gracious, loving person who went about doing good, "formidable" is one of the last words we would think of applying to him.

Yet is there any essential and irreconcilable antagonism between gentleness and formidableness? Is it impossible for these two qualities to exist in one and the same person? If a person's gentleness never becomes formidableness, would that person be anything like a complete person? Would not gentleness that never became formidableness in the face of evil and wrong cease to be a virtue and become rather a contemptible vice? A person who does not become formidable to the wrongdoer can lay no claim to being a perfect person. Now Jesus was meek—but his meekness was not softness. He was gentle—but his gentleness was not a foolish and easy good nature. Jesus was formidable as well as gentle, terrible as well as meek.

The Bible is never afraid of combining seeming opposites in its descriptions of Jesus. It speaks of "the wrath of the Lamb." "Wrath" and "Lamb" do not seem to fit each other. The Lamb is the symbol of patience, meekness, and gentleness, and so has come to stand for the one who went as a Lamb to the slaughter and who "as a sheep before its shearers is dumb, so he opened not his mouth." Wrath would seem to fit a lion rather than a lamb. But the Bible speaks of the "wrath of the Lamb," of the wrath of the one who bore with unmurmuring patience the rude insults and murderous cruelty of evil men. It declares that the gentle and infinitely patient Jesus can blaze out into holy anger. That wrath is the more terrible exactly because it is the wrath of the Lamb.

There is a wonderful completeness about Jesus. There was nothing partial or lopsided about him. We say of certain people that they have the defects of their virtue, by which we mean that if a man is strong he is usually lacking in gentleness and if on the other hand he is gentle he is usually lacking in strength. But there were no defects to detract from our Lord's virtues. Every virtue had its complement. He was gentle and he was strong. He was meek and he was formidable. He would not have been perfect had he been one without the other. He kindled hope in many a despairing heart but he would not have been perfect had he not also inspired fear in the hearts of others.

The Gospels contain a number of examples of this formidableness of Jesus. One example occurred at the beginning of his public ministry when he went to the synagogue in Nazareth and preached. His sermon so enraged the congregation that the service ended in a riot. The people drove him out of the city and took him to the brow of a hill, meaning to throw him off. But when they reached the brow where their murderous intent was to be translated into deed, Jesus turned around and faced them. There was something about him that smote those furious, raging folks to the heart with a sudden awe so that none of them dared stretch out a hand to do him hurt. Instead, he passed through the midst of them and went his way.

Then there is the story of the cleansing of the temple. There were men in the Court of the Gentiles who sold oxen, sheep, and doves; there were others who exchanged the money of the pilgrims for the special money with which the temple dues were paid. It was a profitable business that was carried on with the full consent of the temple authorities who derived a handsome income from it. One day Jesus appeared in their midst, vested with no sort of authority. He was just a young, provincial, undistinguished, and unknown teacher, but he drove the merchants out of the temple and overturned the tables of the money changers so that the coins were scattered about the floor. Although he was only one and they were a multitude, there was something about him so awe-inspiring, so formidable, that they fled helter-skelter out of the temple courts and out of the sight of that face and form before which they seemed to shrivel.

Think of the story of the woman taken in adultery who was dragged before Jesus by a mob of scribes and Pharisees. Jesus at first hung his head for shame, shame for the woman and for the coarse cruelty of the men. But when they continued to clamor for his judgment, he lifted himself up and, looking the brazen men in the face, said, "He that is without sin among you, let him first cast a stone at her." And there was something about the appearance of Jesus just then, some piercing light in his eye, that filled those coarse and brutal men with terror. They wanted to get out of his sight. So, one by one, they slunk silently away, so that Jesus and the sobbing woman were left alone.

Or, recall the story of the soldiers and the temple servants, armed with swords and staves, coming to the Garden of Gethsemane to seize Jesus. He did not wait to be taken. He went forth to meet them at the garden gate and said to them, "Who seek ye?" And when they replied, "Jesus of Nazareth," he answered, "I am he." That self-identification did not lead to them seizing him, though. "When therefore he said unto them, 'I am he,' they went backward and fell to the ground." There was something about Jesus, something so awe-inspiring, something that so struck fear into their hearts, that the mob fell back before him.

We misread Jesus if we fail to note all the features of the Gospel portrait of him, if we think of him simply as the "gentle Jesus." There was always something formidable and even terrifying about him that struck fear into the hearts of evil people and made them eager to escape from his presence.

The formidableness of Jesus was no doubt the formidableness of an absolutely pure and holy person face to face with evil and sinful people. Goodness is always terrifying to evil people. They fear it and shun it. Goodness condemns evil people by revealing them to themselves. That was the reason that Mr. Live Loose gave for wanting Faithful put to death: "He would always be condemning my way."[1] Jesus was formidable to evil people of his day for the very same reason. His very presence in their midst revealed and condemned them and for that cause they hated and feared him.

But there was a deeper and more solemn formidableness about Jesus that is suggested by the words of our text. Jesus quoted these words immediately after speaking the parable of the wicked tenants, which was a parable about Israel, the prophets, and the Messiah. The owner of the vineyard had leased it to tenants and at the appropriate time he sent his servants to collect his agreed-upon portion of the produce. Instead of paying

---

[1] [John Bunyan, *The Pilgrim's Progress from This World to That Which Is to Come; Delivered under the Similitude of a Dream* (1678), part I, "The Sixth Stage."]

the master of the vineyard his due, they mistreated his servants, beating some, stoning some, and killing some. The owner then decided to send his son, for, he said, "They will reverence my son." But when the tenants saw him they said, "This is the heir; come, let us kill him that the inheritance may be ours." So they cast him out of the vineyard and killed him. Nevertheless the vineyard did not become theirs. They were at last cast out and miserably destroyed. Jesus then added this stern and solemn word: "What, then, is this that is written? The stone which the builder rejected, the same is made the head of the corner." And to that he added this searching and almost frightening word of his own: "Everyone that falleth on that stone shall be broken in pieces, but on whomsoever it shall fall, it shall scatter him like dust."

Those who were listening to Jesus knew what he meant. They knew that he addressed the parable to them. They knew that they were the wicked tenants who had killed the servants and were about to consummate their wickedness by killing the Son. Jesus too knew well what was in store for him. He knew that his death was approaching. He knew that in a few days his cause would appear to have gone down in utter defeat and shame. Yet, with the cross confronting him, he told those who were intent on his murder that they could not stop him from arriving at the place that God has destined for him. They might kill him on the cross but he would convert the cross into a throne. They could not get rid of Jesus by putting him to death. The stone that the builders refused would yet be made the head of the corner. Then he went to add the most formidable and menacing part of the saying: "Every one that falleth on this stone shall be broken, but on whomsoever it shall fall, it shall scatter him as dust." Everything and everybody opposed to him would come to disaster.

Jesus was saying that the destiny of people and nations depended on their attitude toward him. People can do two things with Jesus. They can either build on him as a foundation, in which case life becomes strong and fair and secure, or they can collide with him, in which case life gets smashed into ruins. People may rebel against God's purposes but they cannot thwart or defeat them. People may reject Jesus but that is not going to be the end. The most hopeless fight in the world, as Gamaliel well knew, is the fight against God: "If anyone will not make God's purpose the foundation stone for all their living, then the stone becomes an avalanche, grinding them to powder beneath its awful weight."

It is in this fact that the real formidableness of Jesus consists. He is set for the rise and fall of people. He is a stone of stumbling and a rock of offence to all those who reject him, and those who come into collision with him break themselves into pieces.

Now, what is this? Is it a mere theological figment? Is it something to terrify people into submission to Jesus? Or is it deep and eternal truth? If this world is a moral world at all, this is bound to be an eternal truth. If Jesus is the expression of the mind and will of God, then all who come into collision with him are bound to be broken because they are in collision with almighty God. In a moral world, it simply is not safe to fly into the face of truth and justice and holiness. God cannot in the long run be thwarted or defied. The end of the person who tries to do it can be nothing but calamity and disaster.

I am not arguing the matter simply on general principles. The history of the world confirms the warning of our text. This parable was originally spoken to Israel. When Jesus came in sight of Jerusalem on his last journey, he wept over it because he knew that Jerusalem would reject him and that by rejecting him would come into collision with the will of God. Looking down the avenues of the years, he saw doom coming, sure, certain, and terrible. "O Jerusalem, Jerusalem," he cried, "If thou had known the things that pertain unto thy peace, but now they are hid from thine eyes." Jerusalem rejected Jesus. In the finality of their rejection the people clamored for his crucifixion and as they passed beneath the cross they jeered at him and mocked him. They thought that they were finished with Jesus. But in forty years time Jerusalem, amid horrors that defy description, went crashing into ruin before the powerful army of the Roman general Titus. Jerusalem refused the inspiration that might have made it fit to live and in the balances of God it had been tried and found wanting. It had fallen upon the stone and it was broken into pieces.

Or consider the story of Rome. Rome took up the work of persecuting the infant church and trying to stamp out the Christian faith. Rome seemed mighty, impregnable, and eternal. But Rome was also brutal, oppressive, and morally corrupt. John the Seer, looking at Rome and weighing it according to the judgments of Jesus, was sure it could not last. "Fallen, fallen, is Babylon the great," he cried, as if the doom was already accomplished. An empire that, because of its tyranny and cruel selfishness and moral corruption, came into conflict with the moral purposes of God, could not last. And fall Rome did, with a crash that shook the world. It fell upon the stone and was broken to pieces.

This is not only true of nations but also of institutions, social systems, and industrial systems. It is true in international relationships. "Every one that falleth on that stone shall be broken to pieces."

This is also true of individuals. The rejected stone becomes a stone against which we break ourselves in pieces. We do not dwell much on this truth today, but while we may neglect it, we cannot get rid of it. What a person does with Jesus is a matter of great concern. We speak and act as if it does not matter very much whether or not a person accepts Christ. As a simple fact, it matters more than anything else. Those who reject Christ reject goodness, purity, and love and choose instead the base and the evil. They thereby set themselves against the eternal laws of the universe and against God. There can be only one result of such a choice—a broken and shattered life. We can see that truth illustrated in part before our very eyes when we see people who have rejected Christ and the things for which he stands and who experience disaster and ruin.

But it is only in part that we see the ruin here. If this world is to be counted a moral world at all, then there is a judgment coming. Let us not cumber this matter up with questions of the length of the punishment—that secret belongs to God. But judgment and penalty there must be. It is then that the completeness of the disaster will be obvious, when people find themselves in the outer darkness. "Every one that falleth on this stone shall be broken."

What are you going to do with Jesus? It is the critical question. We break or make ourselves upon him. Rejecting him, we break ourselves. But coming to him, the living stone, we get built up into a spiritual house, a holy priesthood, a people for God's own possession.

The Vision
and Compassion of Jesus

But when he saw the multitudes, he was moved with compassion for them, because they were distressed and scattered, as sheep not having a shepherd.   (Matthew 9:36 ASV)

The compassion of Christ was the result of his vision. The main verb of the text is that which is translated "he was moved with compassion" and that verb sets forth the main positive statement of the verse. The grammatical structure of the text makes it clear that the compassion of Jesus was the result of something else. "When he saw the multitudes, he was moved with compassion." The one thing was the consequence of the other. His pity sprang from his perception. His compassion was the result of his vision.

The Vision of Christ

The vision of Christ was the cause of his compassion. "He saw the multitudes." Let me make this clear at the beginning: seeing does not depend simply on the possession of two sound eyes. Otherwise, how do we explain the fact that people see so differently? How is it that the very same sights produce such differing impressions?

Two poets take a walk through the meadow and to one

A primrose by the river's brim,
    A yellow primrose was to him,
        And it was nothing more.

and

To me the meanest flower that blows can give
Thoughts that do often lie too deep for tears.

But another poet says:

Earth's crammed with heaven,
And every common bush afire with God.[1]

---

[1] [William Wordsworth, "Peter Bell: A Tale" (1798); Wordsworth, "Ode: Intimations of Immortality from Recollections of Early Childhood" (1803); and Elizabeth Barrett Browning, *Aurora Leigh*, book 7 (1856).]

Others pass by and they see no gleam of fire in the bush, but simply sit around it and eat blackberries.

One man sees the rising of the sun and for him it is just a disc of fire, something like a twenty-dollar gold piece, but a poet-painter like William Blake sees "an Innumerable company of the Heavenly host crying Holy, Holy, Holy is the Lord God Almighty."[2]

Nothing could be more false than to suggest that what we see depends upon these two eyes of ours and that, if our eyes are equally good, one will see as much as the other.

The fact is that vision is not a faculty of the physical eyes only. What people see depends not just on their eyes but also on their minds, their imaginations, and their hearts. Someone may have eyes that are sound and perfect in every particular, but unless that person has also an imagination and a heart to look out through those eyes, perception will fail.

The secret of our Lord's vision was this: he looked out upon the world with imagination and a perfect sympathy. He not only saw; he perceived. And that is why, when he saw the multitudes, he was "moved with compassion."

If it were true that everyone blessed with sound eyes saw alike, then the sight of the crowd that day ought to have produced the same impression upon all who saw it. The disciples were with Jesus at the time, but we do not read that they were "moved with compassion." It says that only Jesus saw. He was the only one who in the deepest sense saw the crowd. The rest saw heads, bodies, faces, and numbers. Jesus was the only one who truly and really "saw the multitudes."

Do you really see people when you look at a great multitude? What do you see in people as you gaze upon a great crowd at a football game? One day the mighty Persian monarch Xerxes was reviewing his troops as they crossed the Hellespont to invade Greece. As they marched past in seemingly endless regiments and battalions, the monarch's first feeling was one of swelling pride. In those numberless soldiers he saw the evidence and expression of measureless power. Then another feeling seized him. He remembered that in a hundred years there would be not a one left of all those multitudes. He burst into tears. He had seen his multitudes not only in the pomp of their power but as the prey of death.

---

[2][William Blake, "A Vision of the Last Judgement" (1810).]

The remembrance that all are doomed to die is not the only thought that stirs one to sadness as one gazes upon a crowd. What disappointments, what sorrows, what heartbreaks a crowd represents! If we only knew everything about one another, what tragedies would be revealed in our church congregations. "The heart knoweth its own bitterness," says the Bible. And every heart has its bitterness. Business trouble, blighted affections, bereavement, the sorrow and shame caused by sin—they are present in every crowd. The vision of it all in its naked horror would be more than flesh and blood could bear. In his mercy God has veiled it in part from our eyes.

But "Jesus saw the multitudes." He saw not only their faces; he saw their hearts. John said, "He knew what was in man." He walked through life with a vision to which everything was unveiled. He saw the wounds that shame would hide. That was why on occasion he gave way to emotions that startled and amazed the bystanders.

"And when he drew nigh, he saw the city and wept over it." When most of the pilgrims came in sight of Jerusalem they rejoiced and shouted with gladness, but Jesus, when he saw the city, wept over it. The fact was that he was the only one who really saw the city. The others saw its palaces and temple, but Jesus saw the people in their sins and the tragic doom that awaited them. He was the only one who wept because he was the only one who saw. This was one reason Jesus was "a man of sorrows, and acquainted with grief." He saw, as no one else ever saw, the pain and sin and woe of the world.

The disciples were with Jesus but when they saw the throngs they had a feeling of elation. They saw recruits for the Master's cause. They saw a growing army and they rejoiced. But Jesus saw a multitude of men and women bowed down beneath burdens of care and sorrow and sin, and he was stirred to a passion of pity for them. He saw the multitudes, and was moved with compassion.

Vision is still the condition of compassion. There is a vast amount of apathy and unconcern and callousness in our modern society. I do not believe people could go on living in selfish and wanton luxury if they once really saw the need and misery all about them. They are indifferent to the cruel wrongs of life because they do not see them. To be sure, there are a few people so innately selfish that the do not want to see and, if they can possibly avoid it, they will not see. They do not want their peace of mind disturbed; they do not want their consciences aroused. But the great majority who are indifferent and unconcerned are that way because they have never seen the multitude. If you do not see them then it is easy to go on your way not heeding and not caring.

What we need in order to stir us up to service and sacrifice is a clarified vision. We want to see the multitude. I said earlier that it is in mercy that God has drawn a veil over our eyes so that we cannot see all the ghastly tragedies of human souls. Now I want to say that the more we see and the more we seek to see, the more like Christ we become. It is a painful knowledge. But Peter said that Christians are to enter into "the fellowship of Christ's sufferings." A Christian is one who is willing to share Christ's sorrows. Therefore, if we are really anxious to be like Christ, we will make it our business to try to see. We will bring ourselves face to face with the tragic facts of life. When we see people we will think of the burdens, cares, and sorrows they carry. We will train ourselves to see the multitudes as Christ saw them. We will think not only of their circumstances, seeing them in their need and want and sin. We will also, like Jesus, be "moved with compassion," and that compassion in turn will inspire us with our Lord's passion for service. A clarified vision is the condition of an enlarged compassion.

The Compassion of Christ

Let us notice the compassion of Jesus that issued from his vision. "When he saw the multitudes, he was moved with compassion." That word "compassion" is a rich and beautiful word that exactly describes the feelings of Christ when he beheld the multitude. It comes from the Latin and is a compound of two words that literally mean "suffering with." That is exactly what Jesus did when he came across need and distress and pain. He "suffered with" them. He felt the distress and pain as if it were his own. In all their afflictions he was afflicted. He bore their sins and carried their sorrows. He suffered with all sufferers.

There is a sweet monotony in the way this grace of compassion is attributed to Christ in the Gospels. He had a perfect passion for helping, healing, and saving. There was not a single ill under which people suffered that Jesus did not "suffer with" them. Three things especially called out Christ's compassion. I mention them in ascending order: (1) physical need; (2) pain and sorrow; and (3) the ruin and havoc caused by sin. The sight of these things always moved him to compassion.

(1) He was "moved with compassion" for *physical need and want.* "I have compassion on the multitude," he said one day, "because they continue with me now three days and have nothing to eat" (Matthew 15:32). The

sight of the world's poor always stirred our Lord's soul to pity. He knew himself the pinch of poverty. There had not been much to spare in the little home at Nazareth. He had himself endured the pangs of hunger. Our Lord was always "moved with compassion" at the sight of fainting and famished people.

I need not say that Christ's primary business is with the souls of people. He came to seek and to save the lost. He was essentially and principally not a social worker or a reformer but rather a Savior. But I would be giving a totally false impression of our Lord if I implied or allowed you to infer that he had no concern for the physical needs of people. Christ cared not only for the spiritual condition of people but also for the external circumstances in which they lived. He came to preach good tidings to the poor. His own heart was stirred to its depths by the sight of need. His sternest warnings were addressed to people who, like Dives, neglected the poor and needy who were at their gates.

The Christian is bound, like his Lord, to consider the poor. To reduce Christianity to a sort of program of social reform is a grave error on the one side, but to say that it has nothing to do with social reform is to be guilty of as grave an error on the other. The poor are our concern. The fact that millions of our people are living on the borderline—that is our concern. The fact that some are so poor that they cannot bring up their families in decent conditions—that is our concern. The condition of the poor touched the fountains of Christ's pity. We are no followers of his unless the vision of the physical needs of others stirs us also to compassion. Christianity itself is make-believe unless, wherever it is professed, it brings good tidings to the poor.

(2) Our Lord was "moved to compassion" by the vision of *pain and sorrow*. He suffered with every sufferer. It was from his infinite compassion that nearly all his deeds of power sprang. His miracles were the product of his pity. A leper came to him and besought him to set him free from his loathsome disease and Jesus, "moved with compassion," stretched forth his hand and said, "I will, be thou clean."

Two men sat by the wayside at Jericho begging. The crowd tried to silence them when they began to cry out to Jesus for healing. But he commanded them to be brought and "moved with compassion" for those men who were shut out from the vision of God's fair earth and from the sight of their own beloved, he touched their eyes and straightway they received their sight.

Jesus was walking into Nain one day when at the gate he met a funeral procession. It was the funeral of a young man who was the only son of his mother who was a widow. It was a common enough sight, I dare say. But the pathos of it all touched our Lord's heart. He "suffered with" that weeping mother. When the Lord saw her he "had compassion" on her and said to her, "Weep not." And he touched the bier and said, "Young man, I say unto thee, Arise." The young man then sat up and was given back to his mother.

Our Lord was moved with compassion for the poor; he was stirred to an even more profound pity for the suffering and sorrow-stricken. Pain and loss are more tragic evils even than poverty, and our Lord was always quick to minister to those who suffered from them. Whosoever would be a Christian must be like his Lord in this respect: he must have compassion on every wounded person he comes across along life's way. And he must be on the lookout for the wounded one too.

The world is full of grief and loss. Do you constrain yourself sometimes to think of it? We see the halt and lame and blind in our streets. Do you feel the throb of sympathy when you pass them? Does your sympathy prompt you sometimes to say a kind word? We have our hospitals. Do you ever think of the sufferers who lie on the beds and fill the wards? Do you ever think of the people lying there helpless and weak, unable to earn bread for their families? Do you ever think of the mothers lying there, separated from their children? Do you ever think of the little children lying there cut off from the frolic and play of childhood? Is your heart ever moved with compassion as you think of such people? From week to week we meet a funeral procession. Does the sight ever melt you to tears? Do you ever think of the desolate hearts in the cars that pass?

We live in a world of broken and bleeding hearts and while compassion cannot heal disease or snatch the prey from the jaws of death, it is nonetheless a balm for bleeding and broken hearts. If we want to imitate Christ the first thing we must do is to put on a heart of compassion.

(3) Jesus was moved with compassion by the vision of the *havoc and ruin wrought by sin*. That was what stirred him to such a passion of pity as he looked out on the multitudes referred to in the text. It is quite possible that the majority of them belonged to the poorer class. But it was not the thought of their poverty that so deeply moved Christ. And it was not that there were many sick in the crowd. It was the ordinary, everyday, normal sort of multitude. What moved Christ with compassion was their moral condition. They were like sheep without a shepherd. They had wandered away

from the pastures and had gotten lost. Once deprived of the shepherd's oversight and care, they had become exposed to all kinds of perils and disasters. They were "distressed" and "scattered." This was the vision Christ had of this multitude. To the everyday onlooker they were just a crowd of average, respectable, decent men and women. Jesus, who knew what was in the hearts of people, saw them as distressed and scattered sheep.

They were "distressed." The English word does not adequately convey the force of the Greek word that it translates. The Greek work literally means "flayed, torn, mangled." A sheep that went astray usually fell prey to prowling beasts that tore and mangled it. That is how Jesus beheld the people in this crowd: they were flayed, torn, and mangled by sin. Peter said, "The devil, as a roaring lion, walketh about, seeking whom he may devour" (1 Peter 5:8).

The souls of these people had been among lions. They bore the marks of the lions' claws and teeth. They were lacerated, flayed, and torn. They were full of wounds and bruises and festering sores. The lion had laid his claws upon their honor, their truth, their purity, and their good. From many a wounded spirit the cry was going up to God, "Save me from the lion's mouth" (Psalm 22:21).

The people were not only flayed and torn; they were also "scattered." The word "scattered" literally means "thrown down" or "prostrate," either through faintness or famine. It is a picture of a sheep at the last gasp, unable to rise because of weakness. That again is how Jesus beheld the people in the crowd—trampled down, prostrate, and unable to rise. They were sick and helpless and ready to die, for that is what sin does to people. Sin tramples on people as well as tearing and mangling them. It reduces them to helplessness and despair. It robs them of the power to rise. Sin means disablement as well as disfigurement and the disablement, unless rescue comes, is bound to end in death. The helpless sheep is bound to be the wild beast's prey. That is how Jesus saw the people—torn and prostrate, disfigured and disabled, and in consequent danger of death through sin. "And when he saw the multitudes he was moved with compassion because they were mangled and prostrate, as sheep not having a shepherd."

Nothing moved Christ to such pity as the vision of sin. Poverty and pain, in our Lord's view, were not to be dreaded nearly as much as sin. The power for mischief of poverty and pain is limited. Sin's power for evil is infinite and eternal. Poverty and pain for the most part affect the body but sin menaces the soul. Therefore, Christ came into the world primarily to save people from their sins. He came to rescue those who were drawn aside and enticed by their own lusts. He went to the cross because our salvation could not be had in an easier way. He who knew no sin became sin for us. He allowed sin's claws and fangs to fall on him so that the poor, flayed, and prostrate sheep might escape. "The Good Shepherd layeth down his life for the sheep" (John 10:11).

Those who would be Christians must, like their Lord, be "moved with compassion" at the sight of the havoc and ruin of sin. We have an unusual situation today. Our people have become more and more sensitive about poverty and pain but more careless and indifferent about sin. They are more affected by sickness of body than they are about sickness of soul. Philanthropy is more fashionable in many circles than religion. People are more readily persuaded to give to hospitals than they are to missions. They have not seen the multitudes like Jesus saw them! They see the mischief and some of the results of sin but they do not see the deadly secret hurt. Our greatest need is for the recovery of the passion for souls. We need to see the people as Jesus saw them. We must see them lost like a sheep was lost—mangled, prostrate, and at the point of death. Sin rends and tears and defiles and destroys the soul. We are indifferent and callous and unconcerned because we do not see.

If we saw, we would share with Christ the work of seeking the lost and would be willing to become all things to all people so that we could by all means save some.

The Death of Christ

For I delivered unto you first of all that which also I received: that
Christ died for our sins according to the scriptures.

(1 Corinthians 15:3 ASV)

There are some passages of Scripture that it seems almost sacrilege to analyze and discuss. It's like analyzing your mother's face to see what it is that makes that face the fairest in all the world. Of these passages of Scripture surely the story of our Lord's Passion stands preeminent. We cannot help but feel that in the presence of the Cross we would do best simply to worship and adore and let the "old, old story" make its direct and irresistible appeal to the heart.

On the other hand we feel compelled to discuss it because throughout the New Testament the Cross is placed in the forefront and so much is made to depend upon it and flow from it that we are under the intellectual necessity of discovering what Jesus did for people when he suffered and died there. The central position the Cross occupies in the gospel constrains us to seek to understand it and to explain what was accomplished upon it.

We have been taught from earliest childhood that the Cross is vitally and intimately connected with the forgiveness of sin and the salvation of the soul. We cannot help but ask "How?" and "Why?" We want an explanation of this tremendous fact. The Cross was not meant to be a puzzle; it was not meant to be a baffling, hopeless mystery. I believe it is to be understood. No one can read the epistles of Paul or Peter or John without seeing that these apostles all had certain beliefs about what happened on Calvary's hill. The Cross is charged with meaning and significance by all the New Testament writers.

Let us look at the main teachings of the New Testament about the meaning of the death of Christ. But first I want to say two things. First, what I have to say does not profess to be a complete account of the Cross. One of the great mistakes made by Christian theologians has been their readiness to claim completeness for their own particular theory of the atonement. There are many theories of the atonement and all of them have their advocates. The fact is that the Cross embraces them all. The Cross is greater than all of them put together. We may have a true and valid experience of the love of God but the height, depth, length, and breadth of that love surpasses our knowledge. We may have real insight into the meaning of Christ's death, yet the Cross is greater than our vision of it.

Second, before we can understand the Cross at all, we must approach the study of it in the proper spirit. When Paul preached the Cross he found it to be a stumbling block to the Jews and sheer foolishness to the Greeks. To people of a certain spirit the Cross is still an offence. Paul wrote this great word to the Corinthians: "Now the natural man receiveth not the things of the Spirit of God: for they are foolishness unto him; and he cannot know them because they are spiritually judged" (1 Corinthians 2:14). The Cross above everything else is "spiritually judged." To the natural person it is a superfluity; it is foolishness. To appreciate the Cross we need the broken and contrite heart. We need a keen and vivid sense of our own sense. The one who gazes upon the Cross through blinding tears will see the Cross most clearly and will see the farthest into the depths of its meaning.

Consider the central place the cross occupies in the New Testament. [In his hymn-poem "In the Cross of Christ I Glory"] Sir John Bowring said,

All the light of sacred story
Gathers round its head sublime.

And so it does. The Cross is the center of gravity of the New Testament. For proof of this statement notice the space the Gospels devote to the account of our Lord's Passion. Turn to the Book of Acts and the epistles and read the accounts of the apostolic preaching.

Look at this text from the apostle Paul: "I delivered unto you first of all that which I also received: how that Christ died for our sins according to the Scriptures." "First of all"—this took first rank. This was Paul's primary and central message. This had priority and precedence over every other proclamation. From this, as from a fountain, Paul's entire gospel flowed. "First of all . . . Christ died for our sins." "First of all"? Yes, and last of all, too. It was the sum and substance, the alpha and omega, the beginning and end of Paul's teaching and preaching. In the second chapter of this same epistle, Paul said, "For I determined not to know anything among you, save Jesus Christ and him crucified" (1 Cor. 2:2).

Yes, the Cross was central and primary in all Paul's preaching. Upon it he concentrated all the emphasis of his message. "First of all . . . Christ died for our sins."

It was not Paul alone who gave the Cross this central and primary place. In doing so he was following the example of the other apostles who were in Christ before he was. As you read the words of Peter and John and the record of the apostolic preaching in the Acts, you see that Paul and the rest all placed the emphasis on the Cross. Paul in preaching was one with Peter, John, James, and the rest. "Whether then it be I or they, so we preach, and so ye believed" (1 Corinthians 15:11). So *we* preach. And how was that? "First of all . . . Christ died for our sins according to the Scriptures."

The Cross is central to the New Testament. It is the primary fact. It forms the very heart of the Christian message. When we in our preaching and teaching shift the center of gravity from the Cross to something else, then we depart from the New Testament and from apostolic precedent and practice.

Now, what was it that the apostles saw in the Cross that led them to give it this supreme and central place in their preaching?

The Final and Consummate Revelation of the Divine Love

The gospel that the apostles had to preach to the world was, above all things, a "gospel of grace." That was the burden of their message. "For the grace of God hath appeared, bringing salvation" (Titus 2:11). And what is grace? "Grace" stands for the stooping, condescending, unmerited love of God. That was the gospel that the apostles had to proclaim to people—the gospel that God loved them with a deep, strong, free, and infinite love. For final proof of the reality of that love they pointed to the Cross. Love could go no farther than that. "God was in Christ reconciling the world to himself" and to assure wayward, perverse, and sinful people of his love for them he made the supreme and final sacrifice—he suffered, bled, and died for them. Pilate wrote a superscription over the Cross to this effect: "Jesus of Nazareth, King of the Jews." But the apostles wrote another superscription over the Cross of Christ. It is written in a thousand tongues and this is how it reads: "God is love." The Cross, I say, is the supreme and final revelation of the divine love.

All of the apostles see love in the Cross. "Scarcely," wrote the apostle Paul, "for a righteous man will one die: for peradventure for the good man some one would even dare to die. But God commendeth his own love toward us, in that, while we were yet sinners, Christ died for us" (Romans 5:7-8). Notice the collocation "God commendeth his love." How? "Christ died for us." "Herein is love," says that apostle John—here is love at its best and finest and purest—"not that we loved God, but that he loved us, and sent his Son to be the propitiation for our sins" (1 John 4:10). Notice again the statement "God loved us, and sent his Son." The sending of his Son to be the propitiation for sin was the final proof of God's love.

Yes, the Cross stands for love—love whose depth we can never fathom and whose strength we can never measure, love so deep and so strong that it constrains us to sing

Love so amazing, so divine,
Demands my soul, my life, my all.

It is through the revelation of the divine love made on the cross that we know God's heart, God's attitude toward all people. The subduing, overwhelming message of the cross is "God is love."

God and Christ in Scripture are always in perfect agreement. From beginning to end the work of Christ was the work of God himself. God did not need to be propitiated; rather he provided the propitiation. Far from being an angry God who needed to be appeased by the sacrifice of Christ, God himself sent forth Christ in love to die. God was in Christ on the Cross. The Cross is proof, not of Christ's love only, but of the Father's love, too. There is no divorce. "The Son of God loved me," said Paul, "and gave himself for me." Again Paul said, "God commendeth his own love, in that while we were yet sinners Christ died for us." It was the love of God that sent Christ into the world. God so loved the world that he gave. Back of the great sacrifice stands the grace of God. It all originated there. The Cross is the final and consummate proof of the Father's love.

The Divine Judgment upon Sin

The apostles saw in the Cross the divine judgment upon sin. "For what the law could not do," said Paul in one of the most profound passages in his profound letter to the Romans, "in that it was weak through the flesh, God, sending his own Son in the likeness of sinful flesh and for sin, condemned sin in the flesh," or rather, as the Greek puts it, "executed judgment upon sin in the flesh" (Romans 8:3). And what was the judgment God executed upon sin? Death. And such a death—the death of the Cross!

The Cross was God's judgment upon sin. Just because he identified himself with humanity and shared humanity's lot in this world, he had to share in the judgment of sin, and that judgment is seen on the Cross.

In forming your estimate of what that judgment was, do not confine your attention to our Lord's physical suffering. We overstress the physical suffering of Jesus and understress his spiritual anguish. We have talked, for instance, about the "blood" as if the "blood" itself constituted the efficacy of the sacrifice instead of realizing that the blood is the symbol of the outpoured and sacrificed life. And so we have concentrated upon the physical suffering of Christ. But it was not the physical suffering that constituted the awfulness of the Cross. So far as physical torment went, the two thieves probably suffered more than Jesus. It was the spiritual anguish that our Lord passed through that made his death so awful.

Go back to Gethsemane and read how he began to be exceedingly sorrowful even unto death and how he fell into such an agony that his sweat was as great drops of blood falling to the ground. Read on until you come to the point where the deep darkness settled on his soul and he cried, "My God, my God, why hast thou forsaken me?" Who can plumb the depths of that woe? That was God's judgment upon sin.

Paul said, "The wages of sin is death." And what does death mean? Not the mere cessation of physical existence, for in that sense we all die, saint and sinner alike. What, then? For an explanation of "death," you go to the Cross. Jesus "died" for sins. He submitted to becoming forsaken of God for sin. That is death—not the mere ceasing to breathe, but the homelessness of forsakenness and the resultant deep night. Christ endured all of that. He "died," and that death was God's judgment upon sin; it was God's testimony to the enormity and the heinousness of sin. In his own Son, God pronounced judgment upon sin in the flesh.

One of the most deplorable characteristics of our day is the decay of the sense of sin. We have treated sin as if it were a light thing. A French writer wrote, "I have abolished sin." For multitudes of people belief in hell is an exploded superstition. But the Bible does not hold such views. It speaks of the "wrath of God." It describes sin as a terrible and horrible thing. It is impossible to exaggerate its enormity and horror. There is nothing we need to see today more than sin as God sees it. The experience of your heart and mine are one with the Bible as to the heinousness, the enormity, and the awfulness of sin.

But where is the heinousness of sin seen most clearly? The Cross! It is not merely that in the crucifixion of the sinless Christ we see that of which human wickedness is capable. But the Cross itself is God's judgment upon sin. The Cross represents what God thinks of sin. It represents God's estimate of sin. It is God's everlasting testimony against sin. Sin is so awful a thing that the only wages appropriate to it is death. Jesus identified himself with us. He took our sins upon himself when he died. He tasted all the bitterness of forsakenness and homelessness.

Do you want to know what sin is? Come and stand before the Cross. What brought Jesus there? Sin. Sin is a light thing? It laid the Cross on Christ. Sin is a trivial thing? Christ had to die to deliver us from it. Yes, come and stand before the Cross of Christ. In that Cross God passed judgment upon sin. There, if anywhere, the cry will well up from your heart and break from your lips, "God be merciful unto me a sinner!"

The Ground of Pardon and Forgiveness

The apostles saw in the Cross of Christ the ground of pardon and forgiveness. The New Testament writers all agree in making the death of Christ the ground of our forgiveness and acceptance by God. Great difficulties stand in the way of offering an intelligible reason why this should be so, but there can be absolutely no doubt that this is the plain unequivocal teaching of the New Testament. All the apostles agree that when Christ died on the Cross he did something for us that enabled God the Father to forgive sin and bestow eternal life upon people.

What was that something? In some wondrous way, Christ took the consequences of sin upon himself. Listen to this stupendous fact given to us by Paul: "Christ died for our sins" (1 Corinthians 15:3). He "was delivered for our offences," he said in another place (Romans 4:25). He said again, "For he hath made him, who knew no sin, to be sin for us, that we might be made the righteousness of God in him" (2 Corinthians 5:21). "Christ hath redeemed us from the curse of the law, being made a curse for us" (Galatians 3:13).

Peter said the same thing in effect: "Christ also hath once suffered for sins, the just for the unjust, that he might bring us to God" (1 Peter 3:18). In another place he said, "Who his own self bare our sins in his body upon the tree, that we, having died unto sins, might live unto righteousness; by whose stripes ye were healed" (1 Peter 2:24). "Ye were not redeemed," he said in another place, "with corruptible things, like silver and gold, . . . but with the precious blood of Christ, as of a lamb without blemish and without spot" (1 Peter 1:18, 19).

John bore the same testimony: "He is the propitiation for our sins; and not for ours only, but also for the whole world" (1 John 2:2). Later he said, "We are loosed from our sins by the blood" (Revelation1:5). And "By this perceive we the love of God, because he laid down his life for us" (1 John 3:16).

There is but one conclusion from all of this that can be stated in many ways: Jesus Christ on the Cross took our place; the just suffered for the unjust; he bore our sins; he was made sin for us; the result is that we are loosed from sin; we obtained the redemption, even the remission of our sins; we are brought to God; we are made the righteousness of God in him;

the doom of sin fell upon Christ and was exhausted there. The vicarious suffering of Christ for you and for me means union with God.

There is a story of Moravian missionaries to Greenland. These missionaries toiled for many years teaching those people about the Creation, the Fall, the Flood, the Dispersion, and so on, without results. One day, a missionary named John Beck read to them the old story of Christ's love as seen in his death on the Cross. A man named Kayamak, with tears streaming down his cheeks, said, "Tell it to me once more, for I too would be saved." John Beck found the key to the hearts of those people. Wherever the Christ has been presented to people the same results have been obtained. It is the old, old story that we need and desire to hear.

It is the only thing that meets the deepest needs of the heart. It is at the Cross that people find pardon and release. The best of people rest absolutely on the finished work of Christ. One of England's greatest preachers requested that these lines be inscribed on his tomb:

> Nothing in my hand I bring,
> Simply to thy cross I cling.

And that is what I will do: cling to the cross.

> Rock of Ages, cleft for me,
> Let me hide myself in Thee;
> Let the water and the blood,
> From Thy wounded side which flowed,
> Be of sin the double cure,
> Save from wrath and make me pure.

> Could my tears forever flow,
> Could my zeal no languor know,
> These for sin could not atone;
> Thou must save, and Thou alone;
> In my hand no price I bring,
> Simply to Thy cross I cling.

The Resurrection

For I delivered unto you first of all that which also I received, that
Christ died for our sins according to the scriptures; and that he
was buried, and that he rose again the third day according to the
scriptures.   (1 Corinthians 15:3-4 KJV)

When I come to examine the New Testament, I find that what made the
apostles definitely and finally sure that Jesus was the Son of God, the
divinely appointed Messiah, was the Resurrection. He was "declared to be
the Son of God with power," Paul said, "by the resurrection from the dead"
(Romans 1:4). There would have been no Christianity, there would have
been no Christian church, but for the apostolic belief in the Messiahship of
Jesus, and it was the event of the third day that made them sure of it. I am
by no means suggesting that Christ's matchless life had not produced a profound impression upon the disciples. It had. It made them cherish the hope
that he might have been the Messiah. It almost convinced them that he was
the Messiah. But then came the Cross and the grave. Whatever hope they
may have cherished, the Cross shattered. Had things ended at the Cross and
the grave, the world would have heard no suggestion that Jesus was the Son
of God.

But the hope that had been shattered by the cross revived and became
more than a hope; it became a conviction and a certainty as a result of the
happenings of the third day. That is the genesis of the apostolic faith as
Peter described it in his great sermon at Pentecost. "This Jesus," he declared
to the crowd, "did God raise up, whereof we all are witnesses. . . . Let all
the house of Israel therefore know assuredly that God hath made him both
Lord and Christ, this Jesus whom ye crucified" (Acts 2:32, 36). The
apostles' assurance of Christ's messiahship was born of his Resurrection.
By many infallible proofs they saw him alive after his passion and by that
they knew that he was God's everlasting Son.

The fact of the Resurrection is the central and fundamental fact of the
Christian religion. Let us never forget that Christianity is not a speculative
theory; it is not a philosophical theory. It is a factual religion and the central
fact of all is the Resurrection. That is the place the apostle Paul assigns to
it. He says frankly and plainly that the whole fabric of the Christian faith
depends upon the fact of the Resurrection. If Christ be not raised, he
declared, that faith is vain, preaching is vain, the witness of the apostles is

an imposture, the promise of forgiveness is a deceit, and the hope of a beyond is an illusion. In a word, the whole fabric of the Christian religion comes crashing to the ground. As one great writer put it, "If it be proved that no living Christ ever issued from the tomb of Joseph, then that tomb becomes the grave not of a man but of a religion, with all the hopes built on it and all the splendid enthusiasm it has inspired."[1]

It is into the grounds upon which our belief in this central and all-important fact rests that I want now briefly to inquire.

What Is the Fact?

First of all, let us be perfectly clear as to what the fact is. By the resurrection of Jesus the New Testament does not mean simply that his spirit survived death. Many people nowadays are inclined to reduce the Resurrection to the limits of a spiritual resurrection. They tell us that what became of the body of Christ is of no account at all. "If," said Harnack, "the Resurrection meant nothing but that a deceased body of flesh and blood came to life again, we should make short work of this tradition."[2]

Well, no one maintains that that is *all* the Resurrection means. But the New Testament unequivocally asserts that the Resurrection *includes* the raising of the body of Jesus. Like all pious Jews, the disciples believed in the survival of the spirit. They would need no assurance that in that sense Jesus lived after his death. To assert that the Resurrection means nothing more than a spiritual survival is to say that the apostles spent their strength and risked their lives in claiming for Jesus what every one freely granted in the cases of Moses, David, Elijah, Isaiah, and every other good and holy person.

But no one can read the New Testament without seeing that the essence of the Resurrection story is this: that the apostles claimed for Jesus something that differentiated him from every other person, however great and good, in human history, something that put him in a class absolutely by himself. They do not simply say that his spirit survived. That went without saying. What they say is that at a specific point in time, the morning of the

---

[1][Andrew Martin Fairbairn, *Studies in the Life of Christ*, 11th ed. (London: Hodder & Stoughton, 1899) 332].

[2][Adolf von Harnack, *What Is Christianity? Lectures Delivered in the University of Berlin during the Winter Term, 1899–1900*, 2nd ed. rev. (New York: G. P. Putnam's Sons; Longon: Williams & Norgate, 1902, ©1901) 173.]

third day, Jesus himself came back to them. They saw him and spoke to him. They recognized his face and form. People who say that the bodily resurrection does not matter miss the entire point of the narrative. It was not a "subtle spiritual influence" about which the apostles talked. It was not to the helpfulness of such an influence that they felt constrained to bear witness. What they announced to the world—and remember that they risked their lives in the announcing of it—was this: on the third day the grave in Joseph's garden was empty and Jesus himself in the totality of his personality came back to them. That was the stupendous fact upon which the Christian church was founded. That is the stupendous fact upon which it stands to this day.

The Evidence

Seeing that so much depends upon the fact of the Resurrection, it is essential that it should be adequately and sufficiently witnessed. What is the witness for it? Let me offer a brief summary.

The story is told in the four Gospels. They tell us of men and women who saw and talked with Christ after he rose from the dead. They tell us of skeptical folks like Thomas who, by the overwhelming and convincing character of the evidence, were constrained to believe that the stupendous event had actually taken place. You may tell me that there are discrepancies between the various accounts. I freely and frankly admit it. But there is scarcely an event in history that, if examined in the same microscopic way, would not reveal similar divergences. There are strange and startling dis-crepancies, for instance, in the accounts given by the Duke of Wellington, Napoleon, and Marshal Ney, respectively, of the Battle of Waterloo. But no one dreams of making these discrepancies as excuse for refusing to believe that such a battle ever took place. The discrepancies in the Gospel narratives furnish equally little excuse for doubting the fact of the Resurrection that, amid all their differences, all four Gospels unite to assert.

But the stories of the Gospels are not our only or even our oldest witness. Many of the epistles contained in the New Testament were written prior to the Gospels. Take the Pauline letters, for instance. There are two letters, the two to the Thessalonians, that everyone admits to be Paul's own handiwork. There are four others, the great group that includes Galatians, Romans, and 1 and 2 Corinthians, whose authenticity, as Dr. Mackintosh said, no sane critic dreams of challenging.[3] Now, looking at those letters, all of them written between 50 and 60 AD, what do we find? We find that belief in the Resurrection was the belief of the whole church. The story of the empty grave was no myth—as some would have us believe—that came into existence after the lapse of years. Within twenty-five years of the occurrence of the Resurrection we find it accepted as a fact, not for one moment to be doubted, in places as far removed as Galatia, Corinth, and Rome. Wherever the Christian preachers went and wherever Christian communities were to be found, there the Resurrection of Jesus was believed in as a historic fact.

In the chapter from which my text is taken (1 Corinthians 15), Paul gave a précis of the evidence on which belief in this stupendous and un-paralleled fact was based. He did not profess to give all the evidence. The testimony of the women, for instance, was not referenced. I think Paul picked out only that evidence that had, shall I say, apostolic authority.

First, said Paul, Christ was seen by Peter, then by the Twelve, then by more than 500 brethren at once, the greater part of whom were still alive at the time of Paul's writing, then by James, and, last of all, by Paul himself. Nothing could be plainer, simpler, or more straightforward. Paul was writing to keen and quick-witted Greeks. He gave them chapter and verse for their story. He referred by name to men still alive who had seen the Lord after his passion and who could be questioned and cross-examined as to what they had seen. He offered himself for cross-examination, for "last of all," he said, "as to the child untimely born, he appeared to me also" (1 Corinthians 15:8).

What a tremendous witness to the reality of the Resurrection is the conversion of Paul! I know that some say it was only an ecstatic vision that Paul had on the way to Damascus, but the facts put such a suggestion entirely out of court. First of all, Paul himself drew a sharp distinction between what happened on the way to Damascus and the rapturous visions that came to him in the course of his Christian life. These latter came to him again and again, but the appearance of the Lord was given to him but once. Paul attributed his conversion to this signal, unique, objective appearance

---

[3][Probably from William Mackintosh, *The Natural History of the Christian Religion; Being a Study of the Doctrine of Jesus as Developed from Judaism and Converted into Dogma* (New York: Macmillan and Co., 1894).]

of Jesus. He based his claim to be as true an apostle as Peter or James or John on it, for, like they, he had seen the Lord.

In the second place, the psychological condition of Paul at the time makes the suggestion that the Damascus experience was nothing more than a subjective vision absolutely impossible. Visions come to believers, not to unbelievers. They come to men and women when rapt in meditation and adoration. But Paul was on his way to Damascus to persecute. He regarded the faith of the Christians as blasphemy; he hated them as apostates. That such a man should suddenly take to seeing visions of the glorified and living Christ is absurd. Paul did not believe that Christ was alive at all. He believed that, in persecuting Christianity, he was persecuting an imposture and a lie. It must have taken something overwhelmingly impressive and real to arrest Paul in mid-career and to turn the persecutor into a believer. Nothing but a real objective experience, a real appearance of Christ, will satisfy the facts of the case. The conversion of Paul is itself a mighty testimony to the reality of the Resurrection.

Notice, therefore, what we have in the way of evidence. Within twenty-five years of the event, we have thousands of people all over the Mediterranean world persuaded of its reality because they had heard the simple and straightforward story from the lips of people who had seen the Lord. Here are the names given of men who were still alive, who might be questioned and cross-examined by any who were skeptically disposed. Here is the witness of the chief antagonist and persecutor of the Christian church, who said that he was turned from persecuting to preaching because Jesus himself met him along the way.

What are we to say of this evidence? Looking at the mass and weight of it I cannot agree with Harnack that the Resurrection story is an untrustworthy tradition. I find myself endorsing rather the verdict of Hienrich Ewald, a great German scholar of an earlier generation, that "nothing is historically more certain that that Christ rose from the dead and appeared to his own, and that this their vision was the beginning of their new higher faith and of their Christian labors."[4]

The Objection

---

[4][Heinrich Ewald, *The History of Israel*, 8 vols., 4th ed. rev. and corr., ed. and trans. Russell Martineau, J. Estlin Carpenter, and John Frederich Smith (London: Longmans, Green, 1886) 6:69.]

And yet this is the strange situation that faces us, that this fact so fully witnessed, so strongly vouched for, is doubted by some and denied by others. How does this happen? It is part and parcel of the general disbelief in supernaturalism. People who deny the Resurrection do so really on a priori grounds. That is to say, they do not deny the Resurrection because they find the evidence insufficient; they reject and repudiate the evidence because they deny the Resurrection. Or, to put it in a slightly different way, they start from the position that a Resurrection is in the nature of things impossible and so they set themselves to explain away the evidence on which it rests. Strauss, the great German critic, for instance, said quite frankly that he starts from a naturalistic explanation for the Resurrection story, or else his view of the life of Jesus would fall to the ground. This to me is sheer arrogance. When people say that a thing cannot happen because it is against natural law, they are taking for granted that which still needs to be proved, and though they do all of this in the name of science, it is utterly unscientific in method. The true scientific method is to examine the facts and then form a theory, not first to form a theory and then flout and repudiate and deny the facts.

Leaving these theoretical considerations, I want to mention some of the practical difficulties that attend a denial of the Resurrection story. Assuming that Peter, James, the Twelve, the 500, and Paul himself were all mistaken, let us ask what it was that really did happen to Christ. After all, something happened; otherwise the belief in the Resurrection becomes unintelligible. What was that something? We are limited to one of two alternatives. I cannot express them better than Dr. Fairbairn does in his great chapter on the Resurrection in his *Studies in the Life of Christ*. Either (1) Christ died and did not rise, or (2) as the apostles uniformly assert, Christ died and rose again.

I am not forgetting that the older rationalists held a third theory, namely, that Christ did not die but only "swooned." The absurdities of this theory are so great that it has been laughed completely out of court. To begin with, it ignores the strictness of the Roman discipline. It was characteristic of that discipline that, although Jesus was obviously dead, to make assurance doubly sure, the soldier thrust his lance into Jesus' side. The theory assumes that it was the vision of a half-dead Jesus, exhausted, wounded, and with bleeding hands and pierced side, that created in the apostles their exultant belief in his victory over death and sent them forth valiantly to preach his resurrection! The theory is a tissue of wild and silly impossibilities. Strauss himself gave the coup de grace to it. The only marvel is that a theory so monstrously absurd could ever be seriously held by reasonable people at all. In this matter of the Resurrection, we are really shut up to these two alternatives: Christ died and did not rise or Christ died and rose.

The Dilemma

Some say that Christ died but did not rise. Let us inquire into the results and consequences of this position. Before doing so, I ought however to make this remark: scholars of all schools agree that the disciples really believed that a resurrection had taken place. The readiness of the apostles to suffer and die for the faith they preached is quite inexplicable except on the supposition that the disciples really believed that Christ had risen from the dead. The most extreme critics admit the honesty and good faith of the disciples. Their contention is that they were mistaken, that they mistook a subjective experience for an objective fact.

Those critics account for the "mistake" of the disciples in various ways. This is how one of them puts it: "The great myth of Christ's bodily resurrection (revival) is due to the belief on the part of the disciples that such a soul could not become extinct. It was that faith that produced the visions of which the Scriptures record tells us." Others tell us that the visions created the faith. But, one way or another, the vision theory seems to hold the field. Thus, according to Renan, the belief in the Resurrection is simply the result of the creative power of love and enthusiasm. "Heroes," said the imaginative Frenchman, "do not die. . . . This adored Master had filled for some years the little world which pressed around him with joy and with hope. Would people consent to leave him to rot in the tomb?"[5] The empty tomb—how it was emptied no one can tell—helped to make the disciples liable to hallucination. The actual process began with Mary Magdalene. She was an imaginative creature, we are told. In the dim dawn of morning she saw a man in the garden and she imagined it was Jesus. The miracle of love was accomplished and to Mary's vivid imagination and passionate heart the Resurrection became a fact. Mary set an example that was infectious. After she imagined that she had been with Christ, others imagined they saw him,

---

[5][Ernest Renan, *The Apostles*, vol. 2 of *The History of the Origins of Christianity* (7 vols.), first English translation from the 13th French ed. (London: Mathieson & Co., 1890) 2.]

too, until the whole company of disciples imagined they had seen him, and so the stories of the Resurrection appearances arose.

Now let us bring this theory to the test of facts. Before people take to seeing visions, there must be, as indeed the advocates of the theory presuppose, enthusiasm, expectancy, and prepossession. Before anyone could imagine seeing Christ alive, the wish so to see him, the expectation of seeing him, must have already taken possession of the mind. What are the facts in this case? Were the disciples on the tiptoe of expectancy? Were they possessed by the idea that they would see Christ again? Quite the contrary. The temper of the disciples was not one of enthusiasm and expectancy, but of despondency and despair. They gave up everything for lost when they saw Jesus dead on the cross and buried in Joseph's tomb. Even the "imaginative" Mary came to the grave only expecting to find the dead body of Jesus, and when she found the grave empty, all she "imagined" was that, possibly, the gardener had taken the body away. Far from expecting the Resurrection, the disciples were utterly skeptical about it; the reports of the women seemed to them to be but "idle tales." Thomas declined to believe even on the testimony of his fellow disciples. Christ had to reproach them all for their unbelief and hardness of heart. In a word, the temper necessary to make the vision theory possible was conspicuous by its absence from the disciples.

Furthermore, while admitting that it is possible that one person might see a vision, it becomes incredible that a large number of persons, for several weeks and in different places, should be subject to the same hallucination. This theory assumes that the disciples, who were sane and sober men at other times, suddenly took to seeing phantoms. It assumes that these visions ceased just as suddenly as they began. It assumes that, without inquiry, the disciples accepted these visions as realities. It assumes that they accepted from a phantom of their own imagination instructions with regard to their future work in the world. What assumptions these are! And what a tax they put on one's power of belief! Keim says this subjective vision theory is hopeless; he says there must have been some sort of objective appearance. Christ, Keim says, must have given his disciples a kind of telegram from heaven to assure them, after what looked like the crushing overthrow of the cross, that he still lived in glory.[6]

---

[6][Theodor Keim, *The History of Jesus of Nazara. Freely Investigated in Its Connection with the National Life of Israel, and Related in Detail*, 6 vols., trans.

While Keim's theory, by including the supernatural element, comes nearer to the New Testament belief than Renan's, there is one objection that is as fatal to the one as to the other. Every variety of vision theory finds an insurmountable difficulty in the empty grave. We know that within a few weeks of the crucifixion, Peter was preaching in Jerusalem and the burden of his message was this: "This Jesus, whom ye crucified, hath God raised up" (Acts 2:32-36). It is an indisputable fact that the Resurrection was the most prominent topic in the apostolic preaching. How is it, then, if it was only a phantom that the disciples had seen, that the Jews did not crush the entire imposture and deceit by producing the body of Christ?

In the fourth chapter of the Acts we find Peter and John before the Sanhedrin. Peter roundly declared to the Jewish aristocracy gathered there, "Jesus Christ of Nazareth, whom ye crucified, [hath] God raised from the dead" (Acts 4:10). Now, if the appearances of Christ were mere phantasms, his body must have been somewhere. If it was still in Joseph's tomb, why did not the Sanhedrin produce it and so strangle forever the lie the apostles told? They did not produce it because they could not. They could not challenge the apostles' statement because, as a matter of fact, the grave was empty.

Someone may say, "May not the body have been in the hands of the disciples themselves?" But that lands us in difficulties greater still. To begin with, it sacrifices the honesty of the disciples. All admit that they did truly believe in a resurrection. The history of the church is only possible on that assumption; but to assume that they preached a resurrection while all the time the body of Christ was in their possession, is to say, not that they were honest and mistaken, but that they were deliberate, determined, and willful imposters. It is also to say that the apostles suffered, bled, and died for a lie, that they risked liberty and life preaching Christ crucified and risen, while all the time they knew that he was dead. Can anyone conceive such a possibility? Can anyone believe that people, with no selfish advantage to gain, would deliberately risk their lives for what they knew to be false? The thing is utterly incredible! This theory, that Christ died but did not rise, falls to pieces and becomes quite impossible to believe when tested by the facts.

Arthur Ransom and E. M. Geldart (London/Edinburgh: Williams and Norgate, 1876–1883) 6:361.]

The Only Faith

There is only one alternative and that is to believe that the disciples were not mistaken, but that Jesus really died and rose again. Why should it be thought an incredible thing that God should raise the dead? I know that the Resurrection is a stupendous and solitary event, but I need some such stupendous and solitary event to explain the history of the world after the time of Jesus. I have quoted the direct evidence to the fact of the Resurrection already, but the direct evidence is supported by the impressive indirect evidence supplied by the course of later events.

It is only some such stupendous fact as the Resurrection that will account for the change in the disciples. When Christ hung on the cross and lay in the grave, the disciples were a band of broken, disappointed, spiritless men. Shortly afterward, however, we find them hopeful, daring, and fearless. Those timid men, who locked themselves up in the upper room for fear of the Jews, suddenly became as brave as lions and began to bear witness without flinching before governors and kings. They accounted for the change by saying that they had seen the Lord alive. That is a sufficient explanation. Nothing else is.

It is only the fact of the Resurrection that accounts for the changed views of the disciples. Prior to Christ's death, they had dreamed of earthly dominion and material splendor; they had been parochial and narrow in their outlook; the kingdom of God, in all their thinking of it, was to be a restored Israel. But later on, their idea of Christ's kingdom was that of a spiritual kingdom that would embrace the entire world and into which Gentiles as well as Jews were free to enter. What gave these men, steeped in the prejudices of their culture, their new and broader views? The account they give is that Jesus, after his resurrection, gave them their worldwide commission. That will sufficiently account for the change and nothing else will.

It is only the fact of the Resurrection that accounts for the existence of the Church. Had the Cross been the end, the disciples would have been scattered to their homes and the infant Christian society would have dissolved. It was the Resurrection that gave birth to the church and it is the Resurrection that had kept the church alive and thriving. The church lives because Jesus lives. To say that Jesus never rose is to leave the church unexplained. It is to say that the mightiest, noblest, most beneficent society the world has ever seen has a falsity and a lie at the very heart of it. "If this counsel or this work be of men," said Gamaliel long ago, "it will come to nought" (Acts 5:38). If the Resurrection had been a lie, the church would have perished ages ago. I look at this church, which has done so much and suffered so much, which has gone through fire and through water, but against which the gates of hell have never prevailed, which down the centuries has proceeded from strength to strength, and I want to know the secret of her life. The resurrection of Jesus is sufficient explanation and nothing else is.

It is the fact of the Resurrection that accounts for the converting and saving power of the Christian message. Can faith in a dead man save you? No! Faith in a dead man can save no one. But week by week people are being saved in our midst. Week by week people are being regenerated and redeemed. Whose work is it? It is the work of the living Christ. The resurrection of Jesus is sufficient explanation of these stupendous changes and nothing else is.

It is the fact of the Resurrection that accounts for the experiences of Christians. There are people among us who are able to overcome temptation, to fight against sin, to bear trial bravely, and to face sorrow cheerfully. How do they manage it? They themselves say that is by union with a living Savior. "It is all quite true," said one to me, after facing life's bitterest sorrow, "he never leaves us. He has been with *me*." I look at these people in their serenity and cheerfulness and patient endurance.

The fact of the resurrected and living Lord explains it all, but nothing else can. What are you to say to all these things: to the witness of the apostles and the 500, to the change in the twelve, to the conversion of Paul, to the existence of the church, to the Christian Sunday, to the converting power manifested in our midst today, and to the experience of the living Christ possessed by innumerable saints? What are you to say to these things? They are as veritable proofs of our Lord's resurrection to you and to me, just as the sight of the nail prints and the spear gash were to Thomas. The Resurrection is no myth, no fancy, no wild imagination, but a solid fact. Christ went down into the strong man's house and bound him; he has taken death and captivity captive; he lives today to be the friend, brother, and sufficient helper of all who look to him and seek his aid.

Yes, it is all true—"The third day he rose again from the dead." And what shall we do with this Jesus who died and rose again? Can we do less than Thomas did? Can we do anything but fall at his feet and say, "My Lord and my God"?

The Second Advent and Judgment

When the Son of man shall come in his glory, and all the holy angels with him, then shall he sit upon the throne of his glory: and before him shall be gathered all nations: and he shall separate them one from another, as a shepherd divideth his sheep from the goats. (Matthew 25:31-32 KJV)

The Scriptures relate that Jesus ascended to heaven and that he sits on the right hand of God the Father Almighty. From there, he shall come to judge the quick and the dead. The same thing is set forth in the Apostles' Creed. Here we have two statements: (1) that Christ is coming and (2) that this coming is to be associated with judgment.

When I say that the Second Coming and the Judgment are involved in great difficulty and obscurity I am not saying anything that you do not already know. There are some things we know. There are some things we do not know. Many times the candid student must say, "I do not know." Many good people have been led astray by preachers and teachers who went beyond the biblical account. When you go beyond the revelation of God as to the Second Advent of Jesus, you are on your own, you are using your imagination, and you are speculating on what you think will happen. But you don't know.

I recently met a man from a neighboring town. I asked him if he was a Christian and if he belonged to a church. He said that he was a Christian and a Methodist. He said that he did not attend his own church much because they did not give him what he wanted. He said that its preaching and teaching ministry did not satisfy him. So, he said, "I visit all the churches." He added, "You Baptists have a man I like to hear over around Atlanta."

"What is it you like about him?" I asked.

He answered, "He tells me about the book of Revelation. I like that. That is what we need."

In other words, he was interested more in speculations concerning the future than in practicing the Christian ethic. To appropriate the great Christian principles for living was not nearly as important to him as was hearing a preacher rant about some aspects of the future that no one knows anything about. Many of us are that way.

Although many things are hidden from us, we know enough to be able to say, "I believe that Jesus is coming again and that when he comes he will judge the living and the dead."

The Second Advent

Everyone who knows anything about early church history, everyone who has read the New Testament epistles with any attention and care, knows perfectly well that the early Christians lived in the constant and daily expectation of their Lord's return. They scanned the skies morning by morning for the first flaming of his advent feet. They bore up in the face of trouble, scorn, poverty, and persecution, strengthened by the hope that their Lord would soon come back in power and great glory. The awe of it was perpetually upon their spirits; the exultation of it was continually in their hearts. The greatest trial to their faith was the fact that the Lord delayed his coming, that year after year passed and the Lord did not come to vindicate his cause and to glorify his own.

From one point of view, we may say that these early Christians were mistaken, but when we say that, let us be quite clear what we mean. They made no mistake in expecting the Lord to return. The mistake they made was in expecting him to come back in a certain way and at a certain date. If we examine their circumstances we can easily understand how the mistake arose. No one can read the Gospels without seeing that there is considerable confusion of thought in the great eschatological discourses. That confusion, again, is due to the fact that the disciples interpreted all that Jesus said about his return in the light of their preconceived ideas. They had been brought up to believe that the establishment of the Messiah's kingdom would follow immediately upon the revelation of the Messiah's glory. The idea of the realization of the kingdom through a slow ages-long process was entirely foreign to them. When Christ was raised from the dead and thus declared to be the Son of God with power, they expected that the Kingdom of God would immediately appear. The result was that they interpreted everything that Jesus said about his coming in accordance with their traditional beliefs.

There were certain words that our Lord spoke that seemed to give color to their hopes and to justify their expectations. He had said to the High Priest at his trial, "Henceforth ye shall see the Son of Man sitting at the right hand of Power and coming on the clouds of heaven" (Matthew 26:64). He had declared in the hearing of his disciples and a great multitude, "Verily I say unto you, There are some here of them that stand by, which shall in no wise taste of death, till they see the kingdom of God come with power" (Mark 9:1). He had said about John in the hearing of Peter and the other disciples, "If I will that he tarry till I come, what is that to thee?" (John 21:22, 23). He gave to his hearers one day a solemn prediction of his coming for judgment and he gave them certain signs of its approach, so that they might take warning and escape the impending doom. He said it all as if it would come to pass while those who were listening to him were still alive.

There were many sayings of our Lord that gave color to the disciples' expectation of an immediate return. On the other hand there were certain words of his that spoke of his return as a far-off event. The Kingdom of God was like leaven; its realization was a silent and prolonged process. The harvest was at "the end of the world." Of its day and hour no one knew, not even the Son, but the Father only. Such sayings make it quite clear that while the disciples interpreted every word that Christ spoke about his return as referring to that triumphant and immediate return in glory that they had been taught to expect, Christ himself had several returns in his mind. Anyone who reads the Gospels carefully can recognize two or three returns of which Christ spoke.

First of all, he talked of returning in the person and presence of his Spirit. It was with the promise of this return that he comforted the hearts of his disciples on the eve of his passion. "I will not leave you desolate: I come unto you" (John 14:18). He gloriously fulfilled his word on the Day of Pentecost. He came again and he remained with them always. They were conscious of his presence. "At my first defense," said Paul, "no one took my part, but all forsook me. . . . But the Lord stood by me, and strengthened me" (2 Timothy 4:16-17).

Second, Christ returned in striking and subduing fashion in the fall of Jerusalem. No one can read the great eschatological discourse in Matthew 24 without concluding that solemn and awful prediction of a coming in judgment was fulfilled in tragic fashion in the destruction of the Holy City. It is impossible to exaggerate the importance of that historical event. It was God's doom upon the nation that had rejected his Son. It was the great event that finally severed the bonds that united Christianity to Judaism and set it free to undertake its mission to the wide world. That was the "coming" of which Jesus had spoken to the high priest. That was the "coming" of which he had said that there were some alive who would not die until they had seen it.

When we confess with the church throughout the world that Jesus will come again, we mean these two things still. We mean, first of all, that he comes in every movement of his Spirit. When people talk about the Second Coming of Christ, for the most part they think of that catastrophic coming that will bring the present stage of things to its final end. But Christ is continually coming again and we need to have eyes open and heart sensitive to these comings of our Lord. He comes surely in every holy impulse and every good desire. He comes in every softening of the heart and every good resolve of the will. He comes in every pleading of his Spirit. When you feel the call and pull of the higher life during a service of worship, you know that "the Master is come and calleth for thee."

In the third place, Jesus Christ comes in the great events and crises of human history. History is not atheistic to us. We believe Christ is in it. In the great crises that periodically occur he comes in a special and unmistakable way. The fall of Jerusalem was not the only historic coming of our Lord. He came again when the massive fabric of Roman civilization fell before the attacks of Goths and Huns. He came with the birth of modern Europe in the thirteenth century. He came when Martin Luther shook and shattered the edifice of the papacy, brought reality back to religion, and gave spiritual freedom to half a continent. He came at the time of the Evangelical Revival, when John Wesley and George Whitefield aroused a torpid and dead England to spiritual renewal. He came to the United States in the agony of our Civil War. You remember those familiar lines of Julia Ward Howe:

Mine eyes have seen the glory
    of the coming of the Lord;
He is trampling out the vintage
    where the grapes of wrath are stored;
He hath loosed the fateful lightning
    of his terrible swift sword;
His truth is marching on.

I have seen Him in the watch fires
    of a hundred circling camps;
They have builded Him an altar
    in the evening dews and damps;
I can read His righteous sentence
    by the dim and flaring lamps;
His day is marching on.

He has sounded forth the trumpet

> that shall never call retreat;
> He is sifting out the hearts of men
>   before His judgment seat;
> Oh, be swift my soul to answer Him!
>   Be jubilant, my feet!
> Our God is marching on.[1]

And so he comes perpetually to nations. Who knows but that in the crisis of this hour through which the world is passing,[2] the Lord may not be visiting us? History, I repeat, is not atheistic. In all great movements and crises, when the old order changes, giving place to new, whoever has eyes to see may discern the coming of the Son of man.

In the fourth place, Christ is coming again in a visible and personal manner. The Scriptures teach us that Christ will come back to this earth again and will take unto himself his great power and reign. Dr. [James] Denny put it this way: "If we are to retain any relation to the New Testament at all, we must assert the personal return of Christ as Judge of all." The early Christians were not wrong in their hope; they were wrong only in their dates. We too look for the coming of our Lord from heaven. There are some who say that to assert the return of Christ in power is to put "an arbitrary term to the course of history." They say that by a gradual process of growth the Kingdom of God will, in time, realize itself. But there is nothing unethical about belief in the Second Coming of Christ in power and great glory. Dr. [James] Orr said, "There is an inherent fitness, if not a moral necessity, about such a return of Christ at the end of the age as the New Testament uniformly asserts it."

I can see two considerations that make the Second Coming of Christ a matter of morality and rationality as well as a matter of revelation. First, Christ came not just to establish the Kingdom of God but to consummate it. The process of realizing the kingdom has to be completed. Sin and evil are not to be allowed to thwart its progress forever; tares and wheat are only to grow together till harvest. The moral condition of the world is not to be forever that of moral suspense with evil and good balancing each other and perpetually contending for dominion. Righteousness is to spring upon the earth. God is to be all in all. Yet one of the latest and best writers on the

---

[1] ["Battle Hymn of the Republic" (1861) stanzas 1, 2, and 4.]
[2] [This sermon was originally preached at First Baptist Church of West Point, Georgia, on 12 March 1944, thus at the height of World War II.]

social teachings of Christianity has told us that we are bound to recognize that a point may be reached when the forces of human nature will be insufficient to carry the world a step farther on its onward and upward progress. The consummation of the process can only come through some exercise of the supreme power of God. Then and only then will we see the new social order.

And that is exactly what the coming of Christ means. History is not to be a kind of seesaw between good and evil forever. The Lord will vindicate his own cause. The Faithful and the True will ride forth to make war. He is arrayed in a garment sprinkled with blood and his name is called the "Word of God." Out of his mouth proceeds a sharp sword with which he will smite the nations and he will rule them with a rod of iron. He has on his garment and on his thigh a name written: "King of Kings and Lord of Lords." It is this Second Coming of Christ that gives rationality and meaning to the groaning and travail of the world. Unless some such consummation awaits us at the finish, all the agony and striving of the centuries have been in vain, all the blood of the martyrs has been shed in vain, all our struggles and labors have been for naught, and history is bereft of meaning. It is the sure promise of the coming of the Lord that lends meaning to history and that justifies all our labor and conflict and travail. *Maranatha*—the Lord will come.

Evil at last shall fall,
The good shall gain the victory,
And God shall be all in all.

The Coming and Judgment

The second truth contained in the title of this sermon is that the coming of the Lord is associated with judgment. Every coming of the Lord is associated with judgment. Inevitably and necessarily the coming of Christ to any soul is the judgment of that soul. When Christ was here on earth souls were judged by his very coming. "This child," said Simeon to the astonished Mary, "is set for the falling and rising up of many in Israel; and for a sign which is spoken against" (Luke 2:34). And so it came to pass. By his mere presence he divided and separated people. There was a *krisis*, a "judging," wherever Christ appeared. The character of people was revealed. The bias of the soul declared itself. People classified themselves; tried by the touchstone of his character, of their own accord, they took their stand, some on the right and others on the left. "God sent not his Son into the world," said John, "to judge the world," and yet the actual result of his coming was a judgment. "This is the judgment," John went on to say, "that the light is come into the world, and men loved darkness rather than the light, because their works were evil" (John 3:17, 19). He judged the world by his presence in it. The essential goodness of Peter, John, James, and Zacchaeus and the essential evil of the chief priests and scribes were disclosed by contact with Jesus.

Every coming of the Lord involves judgment still. His coming to us as individuals in the appeals and striving of his Spirit implies a judgment. The good heart and the evil heart stand revealed by the answer given to his pleadings and calls. Suppose that at this moment Jesus presented himself to us. Suppose we invite him out of our heart and out of our life; suppose we say to him in effect, "We will not have you to reign over us!" The judgment has taken place! We have declared that evil is good! We have placed ourselves among the goats upon the left hand.

His coming to a nation in the great crises of its history implies and involves a judging. As Lowell said,

> Once to every man and nation
>   comes the moment to decide,
> In the strife of Truth with Falsehood,
>   for the good or evil side;
> Some great cause, God's new Messiah,
>   offering each the bloom or the blight,
> Parts the goats upon the left hand,
>   and the sheep upon the right,
> And the choice goes by forever
>   'twixt that darkness and that light.[3]

The Reformation was a judging time. The Evangelical Revival was a testing time. Some mocked and some sneered; others welcomed those events as great days of the Lord. This time of the Lord's visitation is a testing time. The Lord is visiting America! In the stress and strain of this mighty conflict through which we are passing he is trying the hearts of the people of America. "Who is on the Lord's side, who?" is the challenge he issues to this people. He is sifting us out—the brave and the cowardly, the tepid and the zealous, the good soldiers and the mere camp followers. He

---

[3][James Russell Lowell, "The Present Crisis" (1844) verse 5.]

is judging us all in these searching times. His very presence either condemns or saves us.

While I believe in a continuous and incessant process of judgment, I believe also in a final judgment. I believe that Christ will come again to judge the quick and the dead. That great and final coming will be marked by a "final and definitive judgment." I believe in this, not simply because the Bible asserts it, but again because both reason and justice demand it. The idea behind a final judgment is that at last full, complete, and absolute justice is done. Goodness meets with its due reward; sin meets with its fitting penalty. Now I believe, as I have already stated, that judgment is continuous. God's judicial action begins down here; sin brings its penalty here and now. There is none that leave father or mother or wife or children or lands for Christ's sake and the gospel's but receives a hundredfold more in *this* life. We must not in our thinking postpone judgment entirely till beyond the grave.

No one insisted more strenuously than Jesus that the good or the ill that people do bring a certain reward or inevitable penalty in the enrichment or impoverishment of the soul. At the same time, no one will pretend that full justice is done down here. Take the good person. Every act of goodness, it is true, enlarges the capacity of her soul, but it does not bring her inward satisfaction and peace. The fact is that the better a person is the more deeply conscious she is of her own shortcomings and the more deeply she is pained by them. Why, a good person is often more pained by the recollection of a foolish word or of one unhappy deed than a bad person is by all her deeds of shame. Take the bad person. It is true that sin is punished by a diminished capacity for good but the significant thing is this: that continuance in sin is often marked by a growing callousness and a constantly lessening self-reproach. The penalty, as Dr. Forrest said, is one of loss, not of pain, and "the greatest criminal has the completest immunity from inward retribution." Does not all of this demand another and truer judgment?

Consider another aspect of things. Confine your gaze to this life. Is it not the case that the wicked often seem to flourish like the green bay tree? And is it not also the case that the good often suffer and are martyred for their very goodness? People are fond of quoting Schiller's phrase "The history of the world is the judgment of the world."[4] There is, of course, a

---

[4][Friedrich von Schiller. The oft-quoted phrase is from a lecture in 1789 at Jena

truth in it. But the judgment of the world is a radically inadequate judgment; it does not do justice to the moral claims of the individual. If justice is to be done, if the righteousness of God is to be vindicated, there must be another and final judgment when every soul shall receive what is due to it. And that is the great truth that our Lord asserts when he says that before him will be gathered all the nations and he will separate them from one another as the shepherd separates the sheep from the goats. Then full and perfect justice will be done. The issues of every person's life will be seen. God's righteous government will be vindicated. Sin will be recognized as sin and will find its doom: "Depart from me, ye cursed." Goodness and obedience will be gloriously acknowledged and will meet their reward: "Come ye blessed of my Father, inherit the Kingdom." It is in this final judgment, which the moral order of the world demands, that we express our belief when we say, "From thence he shall come to judge the quick and the dead."

There are many questions about this judgment that could be put to me and that I should find it impossible to answer. One thing, however, is quite clear. The New Testament asserts it and the moral meaning of the world demands it: "We must all appear before the judgment seat of Christ, that everyone may receive the things done in the body according to what we have done, whether it be good or bad" (2 Corinthians 5:10). And this further thing is clear, that, while happiness and bliss beyond thought are the reward of discipleship and loyal obedience, suffering and loss beyond expression are the sure and inevitable penalty of sin. We speculate in these days as to the length of the punishment and the possibility of restoration. Many cherish the faith that God, in the long run, will not be defeated.

> That not one life shall be destroy'd
> Or cast as rubbish to the void,
> When God hath made the pile complete.[5]

It is impossible to dogmatize. The "larger hope," as people term it, is only a "hope" at best. The thing about which the Scriptures leave us in no shadow of doubt is the immense, critical, and decisive influence of this life. Upon the life we live momentous and eternal issues hang. I do not know what may happen in the endless ages of eternity. What I do know is that it is the gentle Christ who tells us that the broad way leads to destruction, that

---

where Schiller was professor of history and philosophy.]
    [5][Alfred, Lord Tennyson, "In Memoriam A. H. H." (1850).]

sin entails the worm that dies not and the fire that is not quenched, and that some go to eternal punishment and some to eternal life.

"You seem, sir," said Mrs. Adams to Dr. Johnson, in one of his despondent hours, when the fear of death and judgment lay heavy upon him, "to forget the merits of our Redeemer."

"Madam," replied Johnson, with his usual blunt honesty, "I do not forget the merits of my Redeemer; but my Redeemer has said that he will set some on his right hand and some on his left."[6]

Yes, my Redeemer has said that, and remembering it, I will divest my message of no shred of its appeal. I am not going to speculate as to what may happen in the dim and distant ages of eternity. What I do know is that sin will be judged. "From the right hand of God, Jesus shall come to judge the quick and the dead." But there is a way to face that judgment without fear. There is now no condemnation to them that are in Christ Jesus. The lovers and friends of Christ do not fear the great and awful day. They love their Lord's appearing.

---

[6][From James Boswell's *The Life of Johnson* (1791).]

Part 2

The Christian Life

Why Be a Christian?

Who is like unto thee, O people saved by the Lord?
(Deuteronomy 33:29 KJV)

There is something like the sound of a trumpet in these words. Surely here we have a word of God to stir and thrill our hearts. It takes religion, the life that is lived with and for God, it takes the life in Christ, and it lifts it up before the eyes of the world and shouts, "Here is the only life in the world worth living." It takes a life that God has redeemed and blessed and regenerated, any such life—it matters not where it is found, whether in the house of God or in the slums—it takes that life and holds it high and challenges the world to produce anything like it. "Bring out your best," it dares the world, "Bring out your very best and highest, and see how that Christ-redeemed life will dwarf it. For there, in the humblest soul on which God has set his seal, is something that you simply cannot achieve, cannot even touch, and never shall." "Who is like unto thee, O people saved by the Lord?"

That is what the word of God declares. Do we agree with it? Certainly it is a daring challenge. It is a vast and sweeping claim. Do you think it is perhaps too daring, too self-assured? Let us look into it. Let us question it. Let us come down to particulars and ask: in what specific ways does the Christian life beat all the rest? Just how is it superior? Clearly, if we can answer this question then the other question—Why be a Christian?—automatically answers itself.

I want to suggest to you four definite points—and there are more—at which the Christian life surpasses every other.

The Christian Life Is Happier than Any Other

Perhaps someone will say, "I find it hard to believe that. To me the Christian life seems cramping, restricting, and forbidding. Did you ever see anything so dull and somber and insipid? The happiest life in the world? I can't believe it!"

It seems foolish that such an argument should have evidence to support it. But it does. There are Christians who, by the dreariness and joylessness of their religion, by its lack of spirit and radiance, are betraying the Master they are pledged to serve, and giving Christ a bad name amongst people.

That is what some of them did for Francis Thompson. He had seen in his youth a good deal of this lackluster religion and he ran off with the thought that Christianity was a prison house and Christ the world's master killjoy. In his own wild words:

> I fled Him, down the nights and down the days;
>   I fled Him, down the arches of the years;
> I fled Him, down the labyrinthine ways
>   Of my own mind; and in the midst of tears
> I hid from Him, and under running laughter.

And he made the reason for his flight from Christ quite explicit:

> Yet was I sore adread.
> Lest, having Him, I must have naught beside.[1]

Today there are thousands holding off from Christ for the very same reason. And what one longs to say to them is this: "Don't be put off by these gloomy caricatures of Christianity. For God's sake don't judge Jesus, the King of joy, by them. Try the real thing, not that miserable parody of the reality. Try the real thing. Make friends with Jesus. Stand where Peter and John and Andrew stood and looked into his eyes. Listen to the music of his voice. Answer his challenge, rise and follow, and you will find it the happiest life in the world."

Look at it this way, if you will. What would you consider to be the three greatest enemies of happiness in this world? I think they are worry, boredom, and self-centeredness.

1. *Worry*. Think of the multitudes who are ridden by it, always conscious of a sword of Damocles hanging above their heads, overwhelmed and overburdened and with no reserves of inner peace, half-hypnotized by life's anxious cares, and totally unable to get free.

2. *Boredom*. Think of the folk for whom life is a listless, zestless, plodding along with never a lift of the heart, never a song on the lips, never a thrill in the soul, never a shout of praise to God for the sheer joy of being alive. There is no "mounting up with wings as eagles" for them. They pass through the world indifferent, apathetic, and bored.

3. *Self-centeredness*. Take the one that is always in the right, always slightly superior, always brooding about others' stupidity, always irritated

----

[1][Francis Thompson, "The Hound of Heaven" (ca. 1888) lines 1-5, 20-21.]

and nervy because he cannot forget himself nor give his critical faculty a rest. The self-centered person never knows what peace means, let alone the deep calm of joy.

So you have these three great enemies of happiness: worry, boredom, and self-centeredness. But now, and this is the point, Christianity slays them all.

1. *Worry*. Christianity finishes that. How? God is on the throne, it says. You are in God the Father's hand, it says. And even though the worst should happen, even though your whole scheme of life were to collapse, even though the very heavens were to crash in ruins, nothing can pluck you, or your dear ones, out of the great Father's keeping.

2. *Boredom*. Christianity finishes that. How? By filling your life with the glory of a friendship whose wonders are unending. Do you think the first disciples were ever bored in the company of Jesus? They were ashamed of themselves often, mystified and puzzled and taken out of their depth quite frequently, sometimes furiously excited, occasionally even frightened. But bored? Never. What a thrilling companion he was! They would have gone through the world with him if he had asked them. And when, after Pentecost, he did ask them, right through the world they went. He is the same thrilling companion still. You never know what romance may happen next, when it is the Christ of God who is with you on the road.

3. *Self-centeredness*. Christianity finishes that. How? By taking you, once and for all, right out of yourself, by sending your critical faculty through the baptism of the Holy Spirit of love. By bursting the petty horizons, and shattering the narrow ways, and thrusting you forth, a crusader with the saints, with Christ going on before.

Think of it: the three greatest enemies of happiness, all slain by Christianity, and buried too deep for any resurrection. And that is the life Jesus offers. "Who is like unto thee, for happiness, O people saved by the Lord?"

There, then, is our first answer to the question "Why be a Christian?" The Christian life is happier than any other. But I can imagine someone saying, "Is that an adequate motive? Might it not indeed be just a species of selfishness to embrace Christianity for the happiness it gives?" Clearly we must attempt a further answer. I ask you now to consider a second point of a totally different kind.

The Christian Life Is Harder than Any Other

Some one may say, "Do you mean that the Christian life is the hardest life in the world? I always thought Christianity was easy, that any one could be a Christian, almost without turning a hair. You just sign your name, you accept a certain theology, you go to church now and then, you say an occasional prayer. Harder, you say? Will you tell me then, precisely what your religion is costing you? Take the past week, the past month, the past year, in what way has professing Christ made things harder for you?"

That is the challenge. Now we have to be quite frank and admit that there is some cause for it, for there is a type of character which turns to Christ's religion for shelter and comfort and for nothing else. It is possible, fatally possible, to worship Jesus without obeying Jesus, like the man who will piously attend dozens of religious meetings and yet be irritable and unkind in his own home. It is possible to sing

Jesus, the very thought of thee,
    With sweetness fills my breast:
But sweeter far thy face to see,
    And in thy presence rest

without having once asked ourselves if there are not things in our life and character that the Holy Presence, if it once came anywhere near us, would burn to shreds. It is possible to take a great bouquet of flowers, an armful of fine sounding phrases, and camouflage the Cross.

I want to put this as strongly as I can: criticize religion if you will, argue it, debate it, cross-question it, but for God's sake don't sentimentalize it. Don't make the name of Jesus of Nazareth sweet or sickly. Don't taint Christ's strong religion with unreality.

One day when Jesus was going down the street, a woman cried after Him, "Blessed be she who bore Thee, and the breast where Thy head lay." But Jesus turned round at once, and rebuked the sentimental speech. "Nay," he exclaimed, "Say rather, blessed are they who hear the Word of God, and do it" (Luke 11:27-28).

A decadent religion may be easy but the real Christian life is definitely harder than any other. Some of our Christian brethren in Europe today have been proving that: for bitter beyond words have been the sacrifices that they have had to face through their brave refusal to acknowledge any king or head of the church but Jesus Christ.

But we do not need to look so far for examples. Every person who is taking Jesus seriously knows that this is fact. It can sometimes be desperately difficult to do the genuine Christian thing.

Think for instance, how Jesus has tightened up the ethical standard.

The world used to say, "If you do not kill or steal or break the social code, that is all that is required of you." Then Jesus came. "I say, No," declared Jesus, "if you have one angry thought, one scornful feeling, one hidden, lurking resentment against your brother, you are sinning against God."

The world said, "If you do not break the seventh commandment, your character will stand." Jesus came and "I say, No" was his ruling. "If so much as one impure desire finds welcome in your heart, even if it is never more than a mere thought, you are sinning against God."

The world said, "If you do just what you are paid for in this life, if you walk the mile that duty demands, you can feel content." "No," cried Jesus, "my religion is to mean more than duty; it is to begin on the other side of duty. What about the extra mile? Are you willing to do that? If not, you are sinning against God."

And so at every point you can see Jesus heightening the moral ideal. Take him seriously and you are in for the hardest life in the world.

"Well surely," says someone in astonishment, "that is a queer reason for recommending Christianity. It is a strange answer to the question 'Why be a Christian?' You have given your case away. It is a first-rate reason for *not* being a Christian."

I wonder. Sometimes the very difficulty of a task is its most magnetic appeal. Is there any young person here who wants the secret of an easy passage through this world? Then you may as well shut your New Testament now and never open it again for you will not find it there. But thank God you do not really want that. You are a far bigger person than that. You want adventure. You are out for a life that will keep you on the stretch. You want a leader who will put you on your mettle every day you live. I offer you Jesus. And for the glory of the hardness of it, "Who is like unto thee, O people saved by the Lord?"

So it is happier than any other life and it is harder than any other life. Will you now take a third factor into consideration?

The Christian Life Is Holier than Any Other

This is a word, it must be admitted, for which many people today have little liking. Ask most people if they would care to be known as "holy" and you will probably get one of two reactions. Either they will laugh at you or else they will be horrified at you. "Holy? No thank you. Anything but that!"

But wait a moment. The word may have lost status in popular parlance but it is worthwhile, as Dr. Fosdick has recently reminded us, to go behind its original meaning. What was that? It meant wholesome and healthy. Holiness means inward health. It means having healthy instincts and healthy emotions; it means having every part of life in a disciplined, balanced, wholesome condition. It means, to put it psychologically, an integrated personality.

Is that not the greatest need of people today? Don't people need something to pull life together and integrate it, to deal drastically with the inward conflicts that damage spiritual health so seriously? Don't they need something to eliminate the discords and repressions and dangerous complexes and to bring everything into harmony and unity? Don't they need something to make them, to use the word it its true meaning, holy?

And why was Jesus called the Great Physician, if not because he alone can produce this kind of vital health? He does that in two ways. First, he gives life a new purpose. That is, he gives a sense of direction, the grip of a great ideal which gathers up all the soul's scattered, turbulent energies, focusing them on one thing. "Seek ye first the Kingdom of God."

Second, Jesus fills life with a new power. That is, he gives a vitalizing, supernatural strength that floods a person's being and sends him out like a conqueror to smash his most stubborn besetting sin, with the light of God in his eyes and the cry upon his lips, "I can do all things through him who strengthens me."

With that purpose and that power, Christ integrates a person. No longer need he pass his days lamenting the burden and the chaos of a sadly divided personality, like the poor pathetic creature in the Gospel, whose name was Legion, for they were many. In Christ, he became a whole person. Emotional health, moral health, and spiritual health were all his. He became "holy." And for this "Who is like unto thee, O people saved by the Lord?"

This life is happier than any other, harder than any other, and holier than any other. Let me make one last claim.

The Christian Life Is More Hopeful than Any Other

Why? Because while every life is bounded by this little world, Christianity has all the windows open towards immortality. Naturalism, speaking in the voice of Bertrand Russell, can only say that no fire, no heroism, no intensity of thought and feeling can preserve an individual life beyond the grave; that all the labors of the ages, all the devotion, all the inspiration, all the noonday brightness of human genius, are destined to extinction in the vast death of the solar system, and that the whole temple of Man's achievement must inevitably he buried beneath the debris of a universe in ruins.[2]

But Christianity sweeps that horror of darkness from its soul and stands facing out towards eternity. And when the day comes which Shakespeare's Prospero foretold, when

> The cloud-capp'd towers, the gorgeous palaces,
> The solemn temples, the great globe itself,
> Yea, all which it inherits, shall dissolve
> And, like this insubstantial pageant faded,
> Leave not a rack behind,[3]

then, declares Christ, then more than ever, the soul of a person will go marching, marching, marching on to God.

There are some today who would take this item out of the Bible, and leave us the rest, some who would banish from our hearts every gleam of glory from the world beyond. They know not what they are doing. Take the eternal hope away and you have no evangel left. "If in this life only we have hope in Christ, we are of all men most miserable" (1 Corinthians 15:19).

No immortality? Then dust and ashes are the goal we are making for. No life everlasting? Then when you said goodbye to your dear one entering the river it was an utterly irrevocable farewell; never will reunion happen, never will the beloved come to your arms again. But oh, thank God for Christ who brings life and immortality to light.

I beg you, every time you think of death and parting, get down on your knees and thank God for Christ. For he has shown you death defeated and parting ended.

O blessed hope! with this elate

---

[2][Bertrand Russell, "A Free Man's Worship" (an essay first published in December 1903), 46-57 in *Mysticism and Logic* (London: George Allen & Unwin, 1917; New York: W. W. Norton, 1929) 46.]

[3][*The Tempest* 4.1.152-56.]

Let not our hearts be desolate,
But, strong in faith, in patience wait
    Until he come.[4]

"Who is like unto thee, O people saved by the Lord?" It is a happier life than any other, a harder life, a holier life, and an infinitely more hopeful life. Why be a Christian? Is any one hesitating? Does someone need just one word more to carry him into the Kingdom? Then let that word be this: it is not only a happy, a hard, a holy, a hopeful life—it is *His* life.

That is what you are being offered—the very life that Jesus lived, the very eternity where Jesus reigns for ever—*His* life. And he is offering it to you himself. To you by name he offers it. Listen, when you say your prayers. Listen, when you are alone and the service of this hour is but a memory. Listen, when your soul is quiet. And it may be that ringing clear through the dark, there will come a voice, and you will hear him speak your name. And then, "Brother, sister," he will say, "I give you this—my life, my spirit, my love and joy and peace—I give them all to you."

What a day tomorrow would be if that happened between your soul and Christ this morning! And how radiant all life's tomorrows, until the last great daybreak comes!

---

[4][George Rawson, "By Christ redeemed, in Christ restored" (1857), #551 in *The Baptist Hymnal for Use in the Church and Home*, new ed. (Valley Forge PA: Judson Press, 1920) verse 4 (6 in 1857 original).]

The Relevancy of the Example of Jesus

Leaving us an example, that ye should follow his steps.

(1 Peter 2:21 KJV)

In these days of unrest, suspicion, and mistrust in national and international relationships, it is fitting to ask the question, "How far is the example of Jesus to be followed as a guide in life today?" Another way to phrase it is, "How far is the example of Jesus relevant to life under our modern conditions?" This is a vital and urgent topic. The adequacy of Jesus and his teaching for modern living is being seriously and widely challenged. People are not challenging the beauty and nobility of the character of Jesus; they are challenging the adequacy of his ethical teaching to meet the needs of complex life in modern times.

Those of us who believe the teaching of our Lord to be adequate and final have no problem. But have we ever asked ourselves why we think it is adequate and final? In what way do we think it adequate in view of the fact that today's world is so vastly different than the world of Christ's day? In what way do we think it adequate in view of the fact that we are confronted by problems that had never risen above the horizon twenty centuries ago? Our belief in the adequacy and finality of the ethical teaching of our Lord may just be an affirmation of tradition but a traditional faith is not a secure faith. All Christians need to be able to offer good reason for their faith in our Lord's authority and sufficiency.

Let me begin by making a distinction between our Lord's example and his ethic. I do not mean that there was any antithesis between the two. Our Lord's life illustrated his ethic. Most of us preach and teach better than we practice. We have to say, "Do as I say, not as I do." We are faulty men and women who are struggling toward an ideal that we have by no means attained. But our Lord's example illustrated his ethic. His life was every bit as noble as his teaching. He told his hearers to be perfect as their heavenly Father was perfect, but he actually was perfect. When I say that we must make a distinction between Jesus' example and his ethic I mean that his example was applicable over a wider field than his ethic and that it is really in his example that we find our Lord's adequacy for all the perplexing problems of our time. Jesus was not primarily a moral teacher but a Savior.

The words of Jesus are wonderful and we would not minimize their importance; in them people find light for their difficulties and the solution for their problems. But the central thing in Christianity is Jesus himself. The Gospels confront us with him; they reveal to us his spirit and it is that spirit revealed in the life of Jesus that is to be our guide in facing the tremendous problems of our time.

Were you to gather together all the ethical precepts of Jesus you would not find in them an answer to all of our ethical problems. In fact, if we want detailed moral advice we would find more in the teachings of Plato and Seneca than we do in the Synoptic Gospels. The Gospels do not give us enough moral precepts of Jesus to furnish the modern Christian with a complete and adequate ethical system. But his example is a greater and wider thing than his teaching and it is in his example that we find all the moral guidance we need.

The example of Jesus is commended to us in two New Testament passages, of which our text is one. In the paragraph from which the text is taken, Peter urged Christian people to be patient when unjustly treated. He backed his appeal with the example of Jesus who, when he was reviled, reviled not in return, and who, when he suffered, did not threaten, but rather committed himself to the one that judges righteously. It is that meek, patient spirit that Peter commends to his readers. In that respect Jesus left us an example that we can follow.

The second passage in which we find this word used is in the account of Jesus washing his disciples' feet. After Jesus had performed the menial task of washing the feet of all of his disciples and had taken his garments and sat down, he asked his disciples if they had understood the meaning of his act. He said, "If I then, your Lord and Master, have washed your feet, ye also ought to wash one another's feet. For I have given you an *example* that ye should do as I have done to you" (John 13:14-15). Obviously Jesus was not directing the disciples to wash someone else's feet at every opportunity. What he was commending was the spirit revealed in the act. The example he called his disciples to imitate was the example of lowly and self-sacrificing service.

It is the spirit of our Lord, not the outward form of his life, that we are to imitate. In its outward conditions our Lord's life was shaped by his calling as Savior. In that respect he is beyond our imitation. But the spirit that animated his life we may all imitate, in degree at any rate. It is in that inner spirit of our Lord's life, in his attitude toward people and God, that we will find our sufficient guide in dealing with the problems that perplex us today.

Let us consider for a moment the difficulties that people have with the ethical teaching of Jesus. I think they are principally twofold. First, people say that our Lord's ethical teaching is inapplicable. Second, they say that there are whole areas of modern life that never come within the range of Christ's teaching at all. Let us consider these.

Is our Lord's teaching inapplicable to our modern life? Let us remember that Jesus spoke in the language of his day, that the questions that he answered were questions that puzzled the people of his day, and that some of the commands he gave were conditioned by circumstances of time and place. So there is an element in his teaching that is local and temporary. Nonetheless, our Lord set forth eternal principles in his answers. We must never forget that in his discourses that are recorded in the Gospels, Jesus was speaking to first-century Jews and not to modern Americans. He spoke to the people who were in front of him. We render artificial the life of Jesus when we suppose that in his sermons he had the people of our generation in view. He spoke to the people in front of him, to their special needs, and to their particular circumstances. When, for example, he gave his instructions to the Twelve as they set out on their missionary journey and told them to take no wallet, no money, and no bread, to be shod with sandals and not to put on two coats, those instructions were obviously conditioned by the circumstances occasioned by ministry in Galilee. They are not to be taken as final instructions for his ministers for all time. There is, to be sure, eternal truth contained even in those words that deal with local circumstances, but in their strictly literal meaning they have ceased to apply.

We must avoid reading back into the documents attitudes that belong to our day if we would interpret the Gospels correctly. We must see them in their proper setting and context and realize that they were spoken to the conditions of Jesus' own day and time.

The second criticism, that our Lord's ethical teaching is not adequate because some of our most baffling and perplexing problems seemed never to have been in his thoughts, is much more serious. Have you noticed in your study of the Scriptures how much of our Lord's moral teaching was given in answer to questions? It was in answer to a question that he gave solemn warning against covetousness. It was in answer to a question that he defined the relations of religion and the state. It was in answer to a question that he gave his teaching about forgiveness. Jesus did not issue a system of ethics. The questions that the people put to Jesus were questions that puzzled them. They were questions that were relevant to their day and time. They did not anticipate our questions and put those to him. If Jesus were here in the flesh today the questions we would put to him would be somewhat different than those put to him by his own people centuries ago. We live in a new world and the problems that confront us had no place in the world of that day.

Let me illustrate it this way. We live in an industrialized world. We live in the age of machines. We live in the age of great factories in which masses of people work for a weekly wage. The industrial revolution, the development of machinery, and the massing of people together for labor purposes have brought with them the most urgent and pressing problems confronting our nation today. This condition did not exist twenty centuries ago. In that day Palestine was for the most part an agricultural country. Life was simple and unsophisticated. No factory chimneys disfigured the landscape. No furnaces dimmed the sky at noon or illumined it at night. The conflict between capital and labor was unknown. Because they were unknown in Christ's day he had nothing to say about them. It would be much easier for us if Jesus had given some specific word telling us how to deal with these new circumstances. But there is no such word! We have to use our brains and think out the problem for ourselves in the light of the spirit we find in Christ.

The same thing is true about our international relationships. The world is a unity in a sense undreamed of in Christ's day. The nations are inter-dependent as never before. What did Christ have to say about protective tariffs, free trade, quotas, and lend-lease? Again, we find no definite and specific word. We have to think out these problems with just his life to guide us. What about the question of peace and war? It cannot be settled by quoting isolated verses of Scripture. We must get our guidance from a con-sideration of Jesus' whole attitude and spirit.

So what can we say about these many problems? Are we left without moral and ethical guidance by Jesus? Must we settle these great questions that confront us by our own wisdom and without any help and guidance from him? By no means! Although Jesus had no specific word to say about economics or about international relationships, I am certain that we must go to him and we must learn of him if we want to settle these questions in the right way. He has left us an example and an example lends itself to far wider application than any precise instruction and rule. By example I do not mean the outward form of our Lord's life but rather the spirit in which he lived and acted toward all people.

No one can stand before the portrait of Jesus as it is given in the Gospels without getting a certain impression of his character and spirit. I see in him a person giving a perfect obedience to God and a perfect love to people. He always did the things that pleased God and he always lavished love upon his fellow people. That is the example that he has left for our imitation. We are to follow in his steps by reproducing his spirit of obedience to God and love for people. We are to imitate his spirit, not his outward circumstances.

We see this truth beautifully illustrated in the way people follow the example of St. Francis of Assisi. That great and good man set in motion currents of feeling that are operative today. Moved by St. Francis's spirit, men and women give themselves today freely and unreservedly to the service of the needy and poor. But it is the spirit and not the outward form of St. Francis's life that they imitate. St. Francis, for example, shockingly neglected his body; we, on the other hand, take great pains to safeguard our health. He forbade the use of books; we build libraries. He embraced lepers; we try to find a cure for leprosy. He changed clothes with an unwashed beggar; we invite such in for a bath. Though they would condemn the precise actions of Francis, the people in our land today who are working to ameliorate poverty, who are fighting disease, and who are engaged in various forms of social service, are really imitating Francis and following his example. It is not by his deeds that a person sets an example but by the whole attitude and spirit of his life. We imitate Francis not by trying to act as he did but by reproducing his spirit of absolute consecration to the service of God and people.

That is how Jesus left us an example. That is the example we are to imitate. The spirit of Jesus, that spirit of utter obedience to God and perfect love for people, touches our life at every point. In him we have all the ethical guidance we need. I believe if we will really take his example and follow in his steps, if we will bring his spirit of obedience and love to bear upon all of our problems, we will find the solution to all of our difficulties. Suppose we apply the example of Jesus to our labor problems. Suppose we tackle them desiring to do the will of God and resolved to practice the law of love to all people. With our minds bathed in that spirit and given direction by that attitude it would not take us long to see our way through.

The same applies to the question of peace and war. Do you doubt that war would be forever ended if people only followed the example of Jesus and were animated by his spirit of obedience to God and love to people?

I say that we find in the spirit of the Lord Jesus Christ all the ethical and moral guidance we need in order to face the complex problems of today.

There are two immense advantages in the fact that it was an example and not an ethical system that Jesus bequeathed to us. The first is that an example expressing itself in a spirit is abidingly applicable. Rules are rigid and inflexible. Rules that suit one age and condition are quite unsuitable for another age with differing conditions. That is why laws become obsolete and new laws become necessary—the world continually changes. If Jesus had promulgated a system of ethics suitable for Jewish life in the first century, it would have been superseded long since. But he gave us not rules but an example expressed in a spirit. That example is universally and abidingly applicable. Paul was right: "the letter killeth, but the spirit giveth life" (2 Corinthians 3:6).

The second immense advantage is this: the way in which the example of Jesus is to be applied to the various problems that confront us will need close and hard thinking on our part. We will have to exercise our brains to discover how, in any particular case, we are to express the very spirit of Jesus. That is not easy to do and some of us would rather be spared that trouble. We would rather be told exactly what to do. We would be as children and some of us would rather be in class forever. God called us to freedom and that includes intellectual freedom. We are to serve God with the mind. It is only as we ourselves grapple with our difficulties and think our way through things and learn to interpret the mind of Christ for ourselves that we develop into full-grown people. If we always have to be told what we are to do then we are babes who have to be fed with milk rather than adults who can eat meat.

Jesus has not left us a complete ethical system but he has given us himself. The example he has left is a sufficient guide for all our difficulties. He is an adequate answer to all our problems. Let us go humbly to him for guidance in all our problems—personal, social, economic, national, and international. If we do, we will make no complaints about his adequacy. We will say of him what Charles Wesley said of him:

Thou, O Christ, art all I want;
    More than all in Thee, I find.

Christ's Easy Yoke

Take my yoke upon you. . . . For my yoke is easy.
(Matthew 11:29, 30 KJV)

In these words of Jesus we are reminded that in those early days he worked in the carpenter's shop at Nazareth. Yokes were widely used in his day and no doubt he made many of them. In the day of Christ yokes consisted of a crossbar of wood with bows of wood at the two ends to go around the necks of the oxen who were to draw the plow or the cart. Travelers tell us that such yokes are common in the Near East even now. To us these yokes would seem to be clumsy contrivances. But it is easy to see that if the yoke did not fit that it would be painful and torturing to the beast. Jesus saw many ill-fitting yokes. He saw the neck of the patient ox chafed and sore because of bad-fitting yokes. Perhaps when he began to make yokes he made up his mind that no badly fitting yoke would ever leave his shop. Perhaps his yokes made him famous among the farmers of his district. Perhaps even at an early age the kindness of his heart showed itself in the care and compassion he had for the cattle that would wear his creation. All the yokes he turned out were good yokes, well fitting and easy.

As the Savior looked upon the people whom he was addressing, they reminded him of those patient oxen he had so often seen straining at the plow or the cart beneath yokes that chafed and galled them. I think it was the pathos of the crowd that Jesus chiefly noticed. He had the faculty of piercing beneath externals and reading the heart. And every time he spoke to people he saw them as a crowd of burdened, anxious, stricken souls. He had compassion on the multitude because they were distressed and scattered as sheep not having a shepherd. Jesus was the only person that ever saw people. He read the heart. And just as he was filled with a compassion towards the toiling oxen that caused him to fashion comfortable yokes for them, so now he is filled with an eager desire to lighten the loads the people before him are carrying. He knew how the load could be lightened. "Take my yoke upon you," he cried to them, "for my yoke is easy."

An Exchange of Yokes

Notice that our Lord invites these people to exchange a galling yoke for an easy one. The great students of the Scriptures tell us that the people wore a kind of triple yoke upon their necks. There was the yoke of the Law, the yoke of Rome, and the yoke of sin. No doubt there were many people that chafed beneath the cruel yoke of Rome. Nationalism is a strange but cruel and volcanic kind of passion. People resent the rule of outsiders and in order to achieve their independence they are willing to lay down their very lives. The people of the province of Galilee felt the dominance of the Roman yoke to be intolerable and were eager to cast it off. But I don't think Jesus was concerned about this yoke when he spoke this word.

The other two yokes are closely allied. The Law with its minute and multitudinous demands was a burden, Jesus himself said, that was too heavy to be borne. And its effect was only to create in people's hearts the consciousness of sin. Remember how Paul puts it in that tremendous seventh chapter of Romans: he would never have known sin, he says, but for the Law. He would not have known coveting except the Law had said, "Thou shalt not covet." The general effect of the Law was to convict him of coming short in this point and that which burdened him with such a sense of shortcoming and sin that he cried: "Wretched man that I am, who shall deliver me from this dead body?" Well, Jesus saw these people bearing the yoke of the Law and incurring only its condemnation and he was filled with pity for them. He invited them to exchange that yoke, the yoke of Moses, for his yoke, the yoke of simple and loving obedience to the will of God. "Take my yoke upon you; my yoke is easy."

Let me stress that point for a moment. It is an exchange of yokes that Jesus invites these people to make. It is an exchange of yokes that he invites us to make today. We all are bearing a yoke of some kind. Don't think that you can rid yourself of yokes altogether. The choice open to us is between an irksome and galling one and an easy one. If we take the yoke to stand for service, then into some kind of service every one of us must enter. To some kind of mastery every one of us must submit. There is in this world no such thing as absolute freedom. We hear a great deal about "emancipation" in these days. By that people mean the flinging aside of old restraints and the repudiation of old prohibitions. But after all these are discarded they have not achieved freedom. They are only exchanging masters—and often for the worse. For the discipline of the moral law is not half as tyrannous as the mastery of the undisciplined self. Sometimes people say that they are going to be their own masters. I hear boys and girls say, "I want to do what I want to do," or "I want to live my life the way I want to live it." Older folks say it meaning that they intend to flout some moral demand. But they don't achieve freedom by being their own masters. The very phrase suggests that they are still beneath a mastery, namely, the mastery of the self, and of all yokes there is none so galling, so intolerable, as that of the self.

To give impulse, appetite, and passion free play looks like freedom, but in reality—as all human experiences proves—it becomes bondage. It brings people under the yoke. In time these impulses and appetites and passions take control; they become our masters, and they tyrannize over us. We cannot break the chains with which they bind us and the yoke they place upon us becomes so galling and so unbearable that people get rid of life itself because they cannot bear it any longer. You must bear some yoke. And in the last resort there are only two yokes to choose between. There is the yoke of self and the yoke of Jesus. The yoke of self may take many shapes. It may take the form of love for money, the love for power, or the lust of the eyes and the lust of the flesh. But at bottom it is always a case of surrendering to the desires of the flesh and of the mind.

Again I say the self is a heavy yoke, proven to be so by life, by history, and by experience. The service of self in any form empties life of its zest and joy. Jesus confronts the world, so full of burdened, unhappy men and women and makes exactly the same appeal to them that he made so long ago to the people of Palestine. "Take my yoke upon you . . . for my yoke is easy."

The art of living does not consist in repudiating all masteries—nobody can do that—but rather in finding the right master. Jesus had found the right one: a service in which he found perfect freedom and which filled his heart with a radiant joy. And he invites us to find our happiness in the same service. "Take my yoke upon you. My yoke is easy."

My Yoke

What did Jesus mean when he said: "My yoke"? That is the yoke he was bearing. What was the yoke Jesus was bearing? His yoke was his loving obedience to his Father's will. Jesus had no will but God's. He had given himself up absolutely to the Father's obedience. He said, "My meat is to do the will of him that sent me and to accomplish his work." He said, "I am come down from heaven not to do mine own will but the will of him that sent me." He said, "I must work the works of him that sent me while it is day." He said, "The night cometh when no man can work."

Many times Jesus was tempted to refuse God's way and take his own way. That was the essence of his temptation in the wilderness. You remember what he said to the devil when he suggested a shortcut to the kingdom: "Thou shalt worship the Lord thy God and him only shalt thou serve." Him only! There were times when the road he had to travel was terribly rough and he would fain have been spared the pain of walking it, but swift upon the expression of his shrinking desire came the cry, "Nevertheless not as I will but as thou wilt." Jesus knew no will but God's and to the doing of it he gave himself in utter surrender. That was the yoke he bore: the yoke of his Father's will.

It startles us, does it not, to hear that it is an easy yoke? Perhaps the word "easy" is not the best translation of the word Christ used. "Kindly" would be better. It was a yoke that fitted and did not chafe. But even the word "kindly" does not take away all our wonder, for we remember what bearing that yoke meant for Jesus. What did it mean? It meant a lowly birth in a manger at Bethlehem. It meant the menace to his infant life and a flight into Egypt. It meant the long years of laborious toil in Nazareth. It meant that during his ministry he had no place to lay his head. It meant that he became the despised and rejected of men. It meant that he had to bear rejection and persecution and scorn. It meant the treachery of Judas and the denial of Peter. It meant the buffeting and spitting in the Judgment Hall. It meant the scourging and the crown of thorns. It meant the Cross with all its torture. And worst of all, it meant going out into the dark night of forsakenness. All of that is what bearing the Father's yoke meant for Jesus. It amazes us to hear Jesus speak of it as an "easy" yoke. Would you not call it a grievous yoke, a heavy yoke, a terrible yoke? Yet Jesus says "Take my yoke upon you . . . my yoke is easy." And when I study the Gospels and see the Master as he bears that yoke I can see that it was a kindly and a congenial yoke.

When we emphasize only the view of Jesus that presents him as a "man of sorrows and acquainted with grief" we take a one-sided view. He was that to be sure but he was also more than that. It is also true that God anointed him with the oil of gladness above his fellows. I think if we could have seen Jesus as the crowds in Palestine saw him we would have seen a radiant kind of Person whose inner joy revealed itself in a shining face. I think Jesus was the happiest man that ever lived—happy in spite of his sorrows, happy in the midst of his sorrows—because he lived in the perpetual enjoyment of his Father's smile and blessing. I believe this gladness of heart was the deepest thing in Jesus. Do you remember the two things he bequeathed to his disciples? He bequeathed them his *peace* and his *joy*. He declared that the world could not give such peace as he possessed and he told his disciples that their joy would be fulfilled, would be really complete, when his joy was in them. So when I think a little more

deeply, I see that this yoke of obedience to his Father that Jesus bore—
though it involved rejection, pain, shame, and death—was nevertheless a
kindly yoke and an easy yoke.

It sounds like a paradox, doesn't it, to say that a yoke may bring you
into all sorts of trouble and yet be an "easy" yoke, that joy can blossom out
of pain, that sorrows may surround and yet a deep and irresistible gladness
fill the soul? But that paradoxical thing is literally true of life. The pursuit
of comfort does not make for real happiness in life—that is the tragic
mistake so many people make. Shakespeare talks about "plucking the
flower of safety" out of the "nettle, danger."[1] And people still pluck the
flower of joy from the nettle of hardship and difficulty and privation. Why
do people find a fascination in trying to explore the remote regions of the
earth, in tramping the forest and jungles and swamps? There are great
dangers to be faced, there are risks to be run, and there are great privations
to be endured.

Think of Admiral Byrd, of what he had to face amid the ice and the
snow and bitter wind, when every step forward was an agony and the hearts
of the members of his party felt as if they would burst! And yet he says
there was a fierce joy in it all of which the man who has chosen the safe and
comfortable way knows nothing at all.

War is a beastly, bloody business. Men faced filth and dirt and cold and
death. They endured hardships and privations of which we can form no conception. Those that believed they were fighting for a cause found a strange
happiness in that holocaust of war and death. A young officer writing home
to his father said, "I feel a strange joy out here. I live amidst mud and filth.
I am familiar with the sights of wounds and death, but I feel that I am living
for something."

It is worthwhile to suffer for a cause. Some time ago a story about one
of our flyers was published that described his feelings. He crashed and as
a result he was lame for life. After returning home to its comforts, back to
making money, back to luxury, somehow he lost the zest and color of life.
Life became flat and stale and unprofitable. He hankered after those days
of terrible hardship, the days when he forgot self at the call of duty, when
he gave blood for a cause, and found that somehow though life was harsh
and grim . . . the yoke was easy.

---

[1]["Out of this nettle, danger, we pluck this flower, safety," *Henry IV, Part I*
2.3.11.]

That lets us into the secret of Christ's word here. There is no cause so exalted as the cause of God's Kingdom. When people give themselves to the service of that cause they are certainly not in for a comfortable time. Jesus was plain, emphatic, and insistent upon that point. He didn't want anyone to be under any mistaken impressions as to what obedience to God entailed. He said: "If any man would come after me, let him deny himself, and take up his cross daily, and follow me" (Luke 9:23). He said we had to "agonize" to get through the "straight gate," and he said it would be a "narrow way" to the finish. He declared that it might be necessary for the kingdom of God's sake to cut off a hand or to pluck out an eye. He told his disciples plainly that in the world they would have tribulation. And yet he said that though obedience to God might entail, indeed would entail, tribulation, denial, and the Cross, people would find the yoke easy. Experience has proven it to be so.

Paul with bleeding back and with his feet fast in the stocks in the inner dungeon in Philippi cannot help but sing at midnight. All his suffering could not quench his gladness. He rejoiced that he was counted worthy to suffer for the Name. His service brought upon him hardships and yet life was a glad and triumphant thing for Paul. It was gloriously worthwhile. He enjoyed it. This is how he sums up his own experience of life: "sorrowful, yet always rejoicing" (2 Corinthians 6:10). Service in the name of Jesus brought him abundant sorrows, and yet through it all he was rejoicing. He was stoned at Lystra, scourged at Philippi, fought with wild beasts at Ephesus, and with all his stripes and imprisonments and shipwrecks his verdict would be "The yoke of Christ is easy." It was easy because it is congenial. It was easy because it is the service for which we were made.

In our hearts we know we are only happy when we are in the service of Christ and doing the will of God. We were not made for the service of self or the world or sin. So long as we are in the service of self we will be restless, dissatisfied, and unhappy—because the deep within us makes continual protest. But in doing the will of God we find our soul's peace and rest. The service of Christ fits us, we were made for it, and as the result we are happy in it. If only this unhappy, disillusioned world of ours would listen to Jesus! If only those poor distracted souls who are frantically seeking their joy in this world's excitements and pleasures, would listen to him! His yoke is easy and bearing his yoke they would find rest unto their souls.

The Yoke Was Always a Double Yoke

The yoke was always a double yoke and it enabled two oxen to share the load and to help each other in the drawing of it. And the yoke Jesus invites you to take is a double yoke. If you or I bear one half of the yoke, he himself bears the other. "Take my yoke." It is a case of partnership. He himself helps our infirmities. He helps us to pull the load and bear the burden. You remember his last command to his disciples, "Go into all the world and preach the Gospel . . . and lo I am with you always." It was a great task, but he was not asking them to do it alone and in their own strength. "Lo I am with you always." If one part of the yoke was on their necks the other was on his. It was a shared yoke.

It is a shared yoke still. Of everything that he asks of you and demands of you he says, "Let's do it together." Perhaps that is why the yoke is easy, because Christ is yoked with us. And we can do all things through him that strengthens us. It is a shared yoke and therefore easy.

But he will not impose this easy yoke upon anyone. He will not fasten it upon your neck. You must take it, take it of our own free will and accord without mental reservation or equivocation of mind. Has anyone ever taken the yoke of Christ and been sorry for it? Has anybody ever entered the service of Jesus, really given himself to God's obedience and regretted it? No, not one! Many have regretted taking upon themselves the yoke of self and sin. They have regretted it with shame and tears and bitter grief. But no one has ever been sorry that he bore the yoke of Christ, that he bore the yoke with Christ. The unanimous testimony of those who have worn the yoke is that it is easy.

Are you restless, unhappy, dissatisfied, and wounded in spirit? Is it because you are carrying the wrong yoke? Is it because you are in the wrong service? Let me assure you and confront you with his call which alone means security, freedom and happiness.

"Take my yoke upon you," he cries. Well, will you take it? His yoke is easy and his burden is light.

Nor Life

Neither death, nor life . . . shall be able to separate us from the love of God. (Romans 8:38, 39 ASV)

What do people really want when they come to church? In the last analysis, I believe people come to church for one thing: to be told of the love of God by people who are sure of it. People long to believe in it. They pray to experience it.

It is this belief that sent me to the words of our text. A braver and more splendid thing was never said about the love of God than Paul says here. It is the kind of assurance we need if we are to face life with all its strange and terrible experiences with a quiet and confident spirit.

[N]either death, nor life, nor angels, nor principalities, nor things present, nor things to come, nor powers, nor height, nor depth, nor any other creature, shall be able to separate us from the love of God, which is in Christ Jesus our Lord. (Romans 8:38-39)

Paul wrote many a glorious and thrilling chapter—the thirteenth of 1 Corinthians and the fifteenth of 1 Corinthians and the third of Ephesians, for example—but I question whether he penned anything more splendid than these closing verses of the eighth chapter of Romans. These verses are quoted by Christians everywhere when confronted by some perplexing Providence or by some shattering grief. For in all the Bible there is no passage more bracing and reassuring than this.

The two words "death" and "life" cover everything we have to face, and Paul says about them, "neither death nor life . . . shall be able to separate us from the love of God which is in Christ Jesus our Lord." It is only in Christ Jesus our Lord that we get to know what the love of God is like. The prophets had only a tiny ray of light as to the love of God. For example, Hosea said God's love for Israel was like a man's love for his wife—it was a love that persisted in spite of unfaithfulness. But we should never have known what the love of God was like in its reach, in its persistence, in its sacrifice, and in its redeeming and forgiving power but for Jesus Christ. It is in him that we see a love that stooped to bear our sins, of a love that condescended to the lowest and the vilest, of a love that forgives until seventy times seven, and of a love that goes after the one lost sheep "until He finds it." It is about that love, the love revealed in the Cross, that Paul makes this tremendous statement: "Neither death nor life . . . shall be able to separate us from" that love. These verses give us our impregnable lines—the great ultimate assurance of faith, behind which we can shelter in perfect security and peace. And that impregnable defense is the love of God which is in Christ Jesus our Lord.

The Ground of Assurance

The implication of the assertion of this text is that to be clasped in the love of God in Christ is to be safe for time and eternity. Notice that it is not our love for God but God's love for us which is the ground of assurance. "Neither death nor life shall be able to separate us from the love of God." Life might seem to separate God from Paul—but it could not separate Paul from God. Let me emphasize this great truth. It is the truth which is the very core and center of Calvinism. We do not do justice to this great truth in these days. We have fastened upon its trimmings, such as its decrees of eternal election and reprobation as if these were the real essence of Calvinism. But they are not. We may dismiss from our thoughts these "eternal decrees." John Calvin in them is the victim of his own logic but life—especially life in God—is larger than human logic. The essential thing in Calvinism, the distinctive thing, is that it starts with God and sets God at the center of things.

Arminianism has a great deal to say about human freedom. Calvinism exalts God in his majesty and grace. Its hope for the world is that God is on the throne and its hope for the individual lies in God's saving and keeping grace. The church and individual Christians need today to come back to this great central truth, for it is eternal truth, and it is the one thing that justifies hope either for the world or for ourselves. I have no hope for the world when I see in it only the conflicting interests and ambitions of human beings! I would despair of it at this hour but for one thing—I remember that God reigns. I would have no hope for myself or others if I relied only on humanity's resolution and determination, for resolution so often falters and determination so often breaks down, but I have every hope when I remember that God is concerned with saving and keeping us. Paul was a mighty man, but this shout of triumph would never have broken from his lips if he had thought only of his own strength and willpower—it was inspired by the thought of God and by the assurance that from God's mighty grasp nothing could separate the surrendered soul.

It is back to Paul's position that we must come if we want to share in his glorious confidence. Our safety depends not on the fact that we have chosen Christ but on the fact that he has chosen us; not on the fact that we hold on to him but on the fact that he holds on to us; not on the fact that we love him, but on the fact that he loves us. If it depended on our frail and fickle wills I would doubt if not despair of our salvation. For our moods vary and dark days come when we seem to lose our hold on God entirely.

Do you not remember that brief, dark moment when our Lord, burdened with the world's sin, seemed to have lost his hold on God. "My God," he cried, "why hast Thou forsaken Me?" Though Jesus for the moment had lost his hold on God, God had not lost his hold on him. Jesus was never more truly the only begotten Son of the Father than when bearing our sins on Calvary, than when he entered that horror of outer darkness. And so it often happens that in dark troubled days we lose our hold on God, but our safety lies in this: that God does not lose his hold on us.

When Oliver Crowell was dying he said, "Faith in the covenant is my only support, and if I believe not, He abides faithful." He trusted, that is to say, not in the fact that he had given himself to God, but that God in Christ had given himself to solemn covenant to him. "I protest," he murmured further, "that I am the poorest wretch that lives but I love God, or rather am beloved of God."[1] "Am beloved of God"—here is the soul's true anchor found, and here is rest secure. We are beloved of God. And God's love neither faints nor fails. Our confidence is not that we have our hand on God but that he has his hand on us. "I am persuaded that neither death nor life shall be able to separate me from the love of God which is in Christ Jesus our Lord."

Death and Life

Let us look for a moment at the first pair of things that Paul asserts shall not be able to separate us from the love of God. "Neither death nor life," he says, shall be able to do it. "Neither death nor life." Does the order strike you as odd? Does it sound like an anticlimax? We would not have written it this way, would we? We would have put it this way: "Neither life nor death."

We would have proceeded from the lesser to the greater peril. But which of the two is the greater peril? Which of the two is more likely to

-----

[1][Samuel Harden Church, *Oliver Cromwell: A History*, commemoration ed. (New York and London: G. P. Putnam's Sons, 1899; c1894) chap. 26, "The Death of Cromwell."]

separate us from God? Death? That is what the Hebrews thought. They thought that at death the soul went to some land of shades unillumined by the light of God's presence. But Christ has abolished death in that sense. Death does not really separate a person from God. It seems to separate a person from his fellows, but not from God. Far from separating a person from God, it unites. It rends the veil between us and the land of which God is the sun. Death admits us to the Father's house. It does not separate between us and him. It brings us closer to him, for we see him face to face. Paul said to depart and to be with Christ is far better.

I do not believe that death is the great separator; I believe life is the great separator. At any rate, we need not worry about death unless we have allowed life to separate us from God. And in any case life comes first. Death cannot separate us unless we have let life do so already. So let us look at life's separating power.

Life

What are the perils in life that seem to separate us from God?

1. *The Zest of Life Itself.* The mere living of life is so full of interest and delight that God and eternal things are apt to be forgotten and ignored. Youth, especially with high-beating heart and with red blood pulsing through every vein, resolves to snatch at the pleasures of life and is apt to find life sufficient in itself. The mere animal life has so many delights and absorbing interests that in the mere zest of living youth tends to dismiss from its thoughts God and the eternal and the spiritual. Life separates us from the love of God.

2. *The Pursuits and Occupations of Life.* Do you remember that word spoken by our Lord about the seed sown on thorny ground? "These are they," he said, "that have heard the word, and the deceitfulness of riches, and the lusts of other things entering in, choke the word, and it becometh unfruitful" (Mark 4:18-19). The cares of the world and the deceitfulness of riches! How true it is! For religion to flourish in the soul there must be cultivation. And some people are so occupied with "things" that they have no time to attend to the interests of the soul. So religion shrivels and decays. "Demas hath forsaken me, having loved this present world" (2 Timothy 4:10). Life's business separates us from God.

3. *Adversity Separates Us from God.* If prosperity tends to make people satisfied with earthly riches, adversity makes people hard and bitter and rebellious and sometimes makes them repudiate God altogether. You remember what Job's wife said when that avalanche of trouble fell upon her

husband! "Curse God!" she said, "and die." She had no use for a God who allowed a righteous man to be crushed by what she thought wanton and unnecessary trouble. The tragedies of the late war had the same sort of effect upon numbers of people. They asked why God didn't stop the war. They didn't want a God who allowed such a catastrophe to overtake his human creatures. I know people who, because of perversity of fortune, because of the failures of their plans and hopes, because of their personal griefs and sorrows, have been driven to doubt and deny God. Life is full of perils of this kind.

Paul knew all this, yet he was confident that life cannot separate us from the love of God. If a person has honestly committed himself to the love of God, if truly and from the heart he has surrendered himself to Christ, that person will be safely guarded and kept amid the trials and troubles of which life is so full. Instead of being conquered by life, we can conquer it. Life shall not be able to separate us from the love of God if we are in the Father's grasp. We can become separated from friends and fortunes and even health. But there is one thing from which various experiences of life can never separate us: it cannot separate us from the love of God. And once we are sure of that, we can stand up to life. We can face anything it may bring—so long as we know we are in the keeping of a love that will not let us go.

Here then is the impregnable line of our faith—this mighty and unfailing love of God. That love in Christ seeks to forgive and keep you. May the Holy Spirit direct every heart into this love of God, "For I am persuaded, that neither death, nor life . . . shall be able to separate us from the love of God, which is in Christ Jesus our Lord."

To See the End

But Peter followed Him afar off, unto the court of the high priest,
and entered in, and sat with the officers, to see the end.
(Matthew 26:58 ASV)

The explosion that shatters the rock and hurls it from its place is the work of a moment; but unseen, often, are men drilling and boring days before in preparation for it. Many of the cataclysms and catastrophes that startle us because of their suddenness have a history. If we could only trace their causes we would find they are not nearly as sudden as they seem. Let's take for example the conversion of Saul of Tarsus. Nothing could have been more sudden than the transformation of this bigoted Pharisee. But was it as sudden as it looked? The vision on the Damascus Road was the explosion that laid his old life in ruins; but when we read the seventh chapter of Romans with its story of spiritual conflict, with its record of Saul's discovery of the inability of the law to bring him the peace he craved for, we see that God for years had been preparing Saul for the mighty change.

It is much like this with Peter's failure. From one point of view the fall of Peter is sudden, unexpected and startling. We thought Peter would be the last one to deny his Lord. He was in many ways the bravest of the twelve; he was devotedly attached to Christ and only a few hours before he had declared himself ready to go with him to prison and death. Yet in the hall of the high priest, at the jest of a serving girl, a ghastly failure takes place. Peter curses and swears that he never knew the Lord. But I do not believe it was as sudden as it looked. Peter's fall had a history. Many things led up to it. Peter's self-confidence was preparing him for that fall. And above everything else his lack of prayer was preparing him for the fall. Our text sets forth a whole catalogue of blunders that Peter committed that led straight to his shameful downfall.

Let's examine some of the mistakes Peter made.

The Line of Communication

"But Peter followed him afar off." Let us keep in mind the fact that all the disciples were seized with fear and in moments of panic took to their heels. They all forsook him and fled. The panic did not last very long with Peter and John. Soon they recovered their courage and followed to watch the developments. That is to Peter's credit. He followed. It speaks well for his affection and his love. But he "followed him afar off." That was his undoing. He allowed the lines of communication to be cut off. We know that if an army allows its line of communications to be cut off it means starvation or surrender.

Peter allowed himself to be cut off from his base of supply. That base was Jesus Christ. There was an endless store of strength and power laid up for him in Jesus Christ. At the side of Christ, in touch with Christ, Peter was brave enough for anything and everything. He had said to Jesus, "Even if I must die with thee, yet will I not deny thee." Peter meant every word that he said. But Peter allowed himself to be cut off and thus put himself at the mercy of his foes. Peter plus the Lord would have been more than a match for his foes. But Peter trusting in his own strength went down to defeat and disgrace in the face of the taunts of a serving maid.

That is the reason for many a fall or defection today. People follow Christ afar off. They do not keep in touch with Christ. They neglect prayer. So long as we keep our hand in the hand of Christ no harm can befall us. So we take life's hardest knocks and experiences. Here are two words we would do well to store in our hearts: "This kind can come forth by nothing save prayer" and "Apart from me, ye can do nothing."

The Danger Zone

The second mistake Peter made was in thrusting himself deliberately into the danger zone. He sat in the very midst of the people against whom he had drawn his sword only a few short hours before. He thrust himself in the way of temptation. The result was he fell badly, shamefully, and tragically.

Our safety against sin lies in being afraid of it. There is a lot of difference between foolhardiness and courage. Those who deliberately thrust themselves in the way of temptation are fools and they are on their own. If you deliberately engage in things that are wrong you do it with your eyes wide open. God only promises to be with us when temptation befalls us in the line of duty.

William of Orange was on a small knoll watching the progress of battle between his troops and the troops of the king of France when he suddenly found a wealthy London merchant by his side. He asked the merchant what he was doing there and whether he knew that he was in a dangerous spot. The merchant replied that it was no more dangerous for him than for the king. The king replied, "True, sir, but duty brings me here; duty does not bring you." Hardly had the words been spoken than a cannon shot laid the merchant dead at the feet of the king. In the moral sphere presumption and penalty follow one another with the inevitability of a law. You cannot live in Sodom without being infected by its sins. Jehoshaphat could not make an alliance with Ahab without sharing in his disaster. Beware of the danger zone. Do not stand in the way of sinners. "The way of the wicked [God] turneth upside down" (Psalm 146:9).

The Weakness of Despair

The third mistake Peter made was that he went to the hall of the high priest to "see the end." He went in a spirit of despair. All his dreams of empire vanished when he saw Jesus in the hands of those cruel men. Peter had lost faith and hope. Despair and denial are twin brothers. If Peter's faith had remained firm he may have weathered the storm.

Faithlessness and failure always go hand in hand. No one will fight for a cause he believes is doomed. No one will fight for a religion that he thinks does not matter or toil and suffer for a Christ who has had his day. Our enthusiasm for Christ is in proportion to our faith in Christ. Some are paralyzed by their doubts and crippled by their fears. We are not quite sure that Christianity is the final and absolute religion. We are not quite sure that the name of Christ is the only name. So we risk nothing, we venture nothing, we dare nothing for Christ and his cause. What church people need today is a quickening of faith and an unwavering and unhesitating faith in Christ. According to our faith shall it be unto us.

The End That Never Comes

Peter sat there to "see the end." But the end he looked for has never come. Yes, they nailed Jesus to a cross. They placed his body in a grave but that was not the last of him. On the morning of the third day Peter found that he had denied God's Messiah, for Jesus was declared to be the Son of God with power by the resurrection from the dead.

The history of Christianity is a rebuke to our hesitancy, faithlessness, and fear. Every Good Friday is followed by an Easter Day. A few days after the crucifixion the apostles were declaring boldly the words of life in the temple. When Rome some two centuries later did its best to destroy the church by horrible persecution by burning its houses of worship, its Bibles, and its adherents, they thought they had seen the end of Christianity. Diocletian and Galerius did their worst but within eight years of that time the cross was blazoned on the banners of the victorious Constantine, and a few years later it was the accepted religion of the Roman Empire.

The Christian faith has proven indestructible before persecution and unbelief. In the eighteenth century Deism held sway in France and England. Bishop Butler said that the people were in agreement that Christianity had been discovered to be fictitious. Within two years of the time Bishop Butler penned those words John Wesley had his heart strangely warmed in a little meetinghouse on Aldersgate Street and then began his mighty ministry that moved England from one end to the other with the result that religion in England was a greater reality than it had ever been before.

Let us take heart. Let us be of good cheer. Let us give ourselves unreservedly to our Lord in prayer and service. Some stand by today to see the end, the end that will never come. There is an end coming and this is it: "Then cometh the end, when He shall deliver up the kingdom to God, even the Father, when he shall have abolished all rule and authority and power. For he must reign until he has put all his enemies under his feet!" (1 Corinthians 15:24-25 ASV).

Let us go on in our labor of love for God and humanity in that faith.

Part 3

The Bible

The Bible as Literature

How sweet are thy words unto my taste!
Yea, sweeter than honey to my mouth!
Through thy precepts I get understanding:
Therefore I hate every false way.   (Psalm 119:103-104 ASV)

The largest and oldest publishing endeavor in the world is Bible publishing.[1] It began as early as the second century AD. Many people suppose that printing preceded publishing but it was in fact the other way around. There was a brisk publishing business in the days of Rome and the Christian church was quick to seize upon it. A thousand copies of a small book could be issued in a month. The method employed was to have one man dictate to a room full of copyists who were usually slaves, who were often, in Roman days, the best-educated people in the community.

Bible publishing stands first in the variety of forms in which the great book has appeared. It has been done on the finest papers and with the costliest bindings. It has been done with every imaginable kind of art embellishment, pictures, illuminated letters, and tooled leather covers. Yet in modern times a copy can be bought for a very reasonable price. It has been printed in big type for children, produced in embossed letters and on talking books for the blind, and has even appeared in comic book form.

The Bible stands first in the number of languages in which it has appeared. Some part of the Bible has been published in hundreds of languages. The Bible is extensively published on every continent. It is published not only in the great industrial cities but also on hundreds of small presses operated by missionaries the world over.

More Bibles are published than any other book. In every year since George Washington died, the Bible has been published in greater numbers in America than any other book. The same is true of many other countries. The great Bible societies publish the vast majority of the Bibles that are produced. Those societies were established by churches of the world for the single purpose of translating, publishing, and distributing the Bible without

---

[1][Dr. Giddens preached this sermon at least three times in observance of Universal Bible Sunday.]

profit and they are determined to keep up the good work until the knowledge of the Lord shall cover the earth as the waters cover the sea.

I want to speak about the Bible, and more particularly our best-known English translation, as great literature. What is it that makes a good book or a great book? A good or a great book is one that affects us in a deep and permanent way. The Bible has moved competent minds in many generations and of many cultures and it must be acknowledged as the world's greatest book.

Simplicity

How does the sacred literature of the Bible excel other literature? The first way is in its simplicity. I do not think that every good book should be so easy that any child can understand it. Metaphysics will remain adult reading however lucidly the writers marshal their arguments and however concrete they make their language. But there are many otherwise good books that fail in this initial requirement. Some time ago I purchased an expensive book because it dealt with a subject in which I was interested. As yet I have not read all of that book and I do not think that I shall read it. Why? Because it is almost unreadable. The author doubtlessly knows his subject—but he cannot write! I find this to be unfortunately true of many religious books. Scholars tell us that this is true of the sacred writings of the East. But it is not true of the Bible.

I do not say that there are no tedious passages in the Bible. There are parts that we read only for special study. The Bible came to us from a time when life was far simpler than it is now. It was written largely in a language that does not lend itself to complexities of style. It is vivid, concrete, and eminently readable. It is so readable that you cannot read it once and lay it aside; you read it only to learn that you must return to it again and again and again. One great student of the New Testament tells us that for a certain purpose he set himself to read the four Gospels every week during the winter. Instead of wearying of the task he read with increasing zest and the last time he read it with keener interest than the first.

I find that to be true in our study of other parts of the Bible. Take the book of Genesis, for example. There are some people who want to abolish it as a collection of outgrown myths. But where can you find greater writing? A sweeter chapter was never written than Genesis 24, which tells how Abraham sent his eldest servant to find a wife for his son and how the wise servant went about his task. A sadder one was never written than Genesis 27, which tells how the elderly Isaac proposed to give his last blessing to his eldest son Esau but, due to the deceit of his own wife, he gave it instead to his younger son Jacob. Apart from the questions of divine inspiration or religious value, can you find many chapters in the Bible worthy of comparison? But if you agree that those two are great chapters, you will have to find other superlatives to describe other chapters such as Genesis 22 that tells of the trial of Abraham's faith and of his willingness to offer his son Isaac as a sacrifice to the Lord. No wonder that Arthur Mee said of these and other chapters

> There are no stories like them anywhere. There is nothing more wistful than the story of Ruth. There are no friends in history more wonderful than Jonathan and David. There is no poetry like the Psalms. There is no prose like Isaiah. There is no drama like Job. If we think of the Bible as only a treasure-house of literature it has never been equaled since books began.[2]

Sublimity

Another mark of good literature is sublimity or beauty. Without any attempt to define beauty or to discuss sublimity and without any comparison with other secular or sacred books, let me give a few examples.

> Thine, O Lord, is the greatness, and the power, and the glory, and the victory, and the majesty: for all that is in the heaven and in the earth is thine. . . . and thou art exalted as head over all.
> (1 Chronicles 29:11)

> Although the fig tree shall not blossom, neither shall fruit be in the vines: the labor of the olive shall fail, and the fields shall yield no meat; the flock shall be cut off from the fold, and there shall be no herd in the stalls; yet I will rejoice in the Lord, I will joy in the God of my salvation. (Habakkuk 3:17-18)

> For ye are not come unto the mount that might be touched, and that burned with fire, nor unto blackness, and darkness, and tempest, . . .

---

[2][Arthur Mee (1875–1943—not his close contemporary, the astronomer Arthur Mee) was a British journalist and educator—and a Baptist. A prolific editor/author he probably is best known for *The Children's Encyclopedia: The Greatest Book in the World in Its Own Words* (1924). Dr. Giddens probably got this quotation from Mee's introduction to that book.]

and the voice of words. But ye are come unto Mount Sion, and unto the city of the living God, the heavenly Jerusalem, and to an innumerable company of angels: to the general assembly, and church of the first born, which are written in heaven, and to God the Judge of all, and to the spirits of just men made perfect, and to Jesus the mediator of the new covenant and to the blood of sprinkling, that speaketh better things than that of Abel.

(Hebrews 12:18-24)

What are these which are arrayed in white robes? And whence came they? . . . These are they which came of great tribulation, and have washed their robes, and made them white in the blood of the Lamb. Therefore are they before the throne of God, and serve him day and night in his temple; and he that sitteth on the throne shall dwell almong them. They shall hunger no more, neither thirst any more, neither shall the sun light on them, nor any heat. For the Lamb which is in the midst of the throne, shall feed them, and shall lead them unto living fountains of waters: and God shall wipe away all tears from their eyes.   (Revelation 7:13-17)

No wonder the great masters of the English language have steeped themselves in the King James Version! I wish we had time to tell the story of these great men and women but one must suffice. During the spring of 1918 when the Great War was coming to a close and the civilized world was rocking on its foundations, Sir Arthur Quiller-Couch, a professor of English in Cambridge University, gathered some of his students around him and talked to them about some things that could not be shaken. In the course of his lecture he quoted some of the great passages from Isaiah and then he said:

The Authorized Version [King James Version], setting a seal on all, set a seal on our national style, thinking and speaking. It has cadences homely and sublime, yet so harmonizes them that the voice is always one. Simple men—holy and humble men of heart like Isaak Walton or Bunyan—have their lips touched and speak to the homelier tune. Proud men, scholars,—Milton, Sir Thomas Browne—practice the rolling Latin sentence; but upon the rhythms of our Bible they, too, fall back. . . . The precise man Addison cannot excel one parable in brevity or in heavenly clarity. . . . The Bible controls its enemy Gibbon as surely as it haunts the curious music of a light sentence of Thackeray's. It is in everything we see, hear, feel, because it is in us, in our blood.[3]

Eternal Truth

As important as readableness and sublimity are to good literature, you cannot separate style from matter. It is not much good to have a thing well said if it is not worth saying. A good book is a true book—true to life—just as a good picture is a true picture. It must be a transcript of reality.

No book deals as the Bible does with essential facts. You may get more accurate science elsewhere. But the essential facts are not scientific facts. That is to say that there are things more important than knowledge of the creation of worlds and the development of the human race.

The essential facts are God and the soul. There are the obvious and persistent facts of humanity's sin. There is the downward pull toward evil and the upward pull toward beauty, truth, goodness, and love that will not let us rest content on lower levels. There is the fact of conscience at which some people may laugh but that is nonetheless a reality. There is the fact of sudden inspiration, when something stabs the soul wide awake, and everything is changed for us forever. There is the meeting of the soul with the Supreme Reality, the living God, the inexplicable assurance that "God is in this place and I knew it not," the desire to take the shoes from off one's feet, for the ground whereon one stands is holy ground.

These are the essential facts about a person's life. The books that live from one generation to another, because they are real books, deal with these incalculable qualities, although in a partial and unsatisfactory manner. But there is one book that in all this has an unchallenged and an unchallengeable place—the book we call the Bible. It stands alone in its manifestation of God's comfort. The living God who in the beginning created the heavens and the earth is in the loving God who sent his Son to be the Savior of the world.

Ought not this book to be in our hands from childhood to old age? Ought it not to be with us in the secret place and reverenced in our homes and expounded in our churches? Ought it not to be the inspiration of all

---

[3][Arthur Thomas Quiller-Couch, "On the Capital Difficulty of Prose" (Thursday 15 May 1914), lecture 6, in *On the Art of Writing: Lectures Delivered in the University of Cambridge, 1913–1914* (Cambridge UK: Cambridge University Press, 1916).]

lessons and the foundation of all education? Can you not understand how the Psalmist, thinking of a part of it only, said that its words were sweeter than honey to his mouth and that the Great Apostle, thinking of him who in a special sense is the Word of God, said he was prepared to know nothing among people but Jesus Christ and him crucified?

Let people take their choice but let them realize that they are choosing a character and a civilization. Let us take our choice and choose deliberately to know "the holy Scriptures which are able to make thee wise unto salvation" (2 Timothy 3:15).

The Textbook of Human Liberty

This book of the law shall not depart out of thy mouth, but thou shalt meditate therein day and night, that thou mayest observe to do according to all that is written therein: for then thou shalt make thy way prosperous, and then thou shalt have good success.

(Joshua 1:8)

Recently an outstanding Englishman made an astonishing suggestion. He suggested that the day of reading is drawing to a close. In the beginning people managed without it. They trusted to gradation and rite and trained their memory to retain what they heard and saw, and books were unknown. Now, with the coming of radio and television and movies, reading may become only the hobby of old-fashioned people and the serious student. It is possible, at least, that the new inventions may destroy the inherited culture of the ages and that the very knowledge of reading and writing may disappear from the world. This great Englishman says that it is happening already. The picture show is more popular than the bookstore and the library combined. And where once families settled themselves to an evening with favorite authors and communed with great minds through the medium of books, now they listen to whatever they can get over radio.

If there is any truth in this suggestion it indicates a revolution of unspeakable magnitude. For ever since humans became able to read and write, books have had a tremendous influence. When you begin to study the records of the past, one of the first things that strikes you is the power of prominent personalities. A Caesar, an Alexander, a Napoleon marches on to the stage and dominates it. There may be many more interesting characters, but these people of action play the principal role and determine the course of events. But when you look more closely you discover that, more than they could know, those commanding personalities are the servants of unseen forces. You discover that as often as not they received their inspiration from the spoken or written word of a lonely thinker.

Keys to History

History has been written in many ways. It has been written as a record of kings and princes, as a succession of decisive battles, as the story of the common people, and more recently as the result of economic pressures. I would like someone to write it is as influences by great thinkers and great books. You can imagine how the history of the Hebrews would shape itself. You can mention at once some of the outstanding names in the most creative period of Greece. You can see how one book dominates the whole story of the Muslim world. When you come to Christianity you want to speak at once of great writers beginning with the Apostle Paul, going on through Augustine with his *Confessions* and his *City of God*, then on to Calvin with his masterful *Institutes*, to poets like Dante and Milton, and to plain writers for a simple public like Bunyan. These are the key individuals, not the cardinals and bishops or the presidents of conventions, but the often persecuted and the sometimes obscure dreamers and thinkers and makers of books.

It is the same in secular affairs. The whole world still talks about Hitler and Mussolini and the smaller fry. Hardly a day passes that the name of Stalin is not mentioned by our press and radio. Behind all these men stands a succession of creative thinkers. Behind Stalin is Lenin, and behind Lenin Marx, and behind Marx Proudhon. Behind the dictators of Germany and Italy and other countries are Nietzsche and Bergson and Sorel and Hegel and Machiavelli. No wonder it has been said that the individual engagements are won by men of action, but the campaigns are won by the thinkers. No wonder Erasmus said that if a good book came to hand he would rather pawn his coat than not obtain it, "especially" he said, and note this well, "if it be religious, such as a Psalter or a gospel."

We make great claims for the Bible. We claim that it is the greatest literature in the English language and that it is the people's book, that it has wider appeal and a securer place in people's affections than any other writings. Now we claim for it a greater influence. It has not only a circulation far greater than any other book; it has made more outstanding personalities and shaped more historic movements than any other book. Was it not Coleridge who advised young men and women to sell their beds and buy books? Surely we ought to advise them to sell beds and blankets, too, to buy Bibles and books that expound the Bible.

The Bible and Social Reforms

The evidence for this great claim is written in the records of the past and in the hearts of those now living. All we can do here is to make one or two points. I wish that someone would write a book on the Bible as the instrument of social reform. He would have to point out that where you have a dominant church but a prohibited Bible you expect and usually find ignorance, reaction, and tyranny and that where you have a prohibited Bible and an persecuted church—as has been the case in Russia—you expect either anarchy or soul-restoring license and you certainly fail to find any reverence for individual life. But where you have a free church and an open Bible you expect to find liberty and progress.

We are proud of the great contribution made to the world by evangelical Christianity. Yet amongst us, in our own times, we have seen idols raised and many tragic consequences have followed. We have seen people neglecting the worship of the living God to serve in the temples of Mars and Mammon. We have paid a tragic price in blood because of our worship of Mars. We have paid the tragic price of civil strife with its attendant evils because we worship at the feet of Mammon. America's god today is not the Father of our Lord Jesus Christ but the almighty dollar. These tragedies and miseries are ours not because the Bible has been prohibited but because it has been neglected. No president of the United States has said, "Thou shalt not read this Holy Book," but the public mind has been distracted and led off to other and less-valuable things.

The remedy is to return to the Book that gives the true values and the eternal standards. No one can be a sincere and discerning student of this Word of Life and remain content with the evils that cripple and destroy us. Who can take this Book and read the story of John's vision of the Holy City in which there is no sin, no filth, no poverty, and no sorrow, and then pass to any city with its slums and red-light houses, its roadhouses and saloons, its tawdry amusements, and not feel profoundly discontented? Who can read the Sermon on the Mount and drink in the Spirit of Jesus Christ and then go to many of our places of business and politics and not sense the glaring contrast? Nothing can shake us out of our complacency and rouse us to activity more than a sane study of the Scriptures. It has happened before. People have come to and have read this Book and a power not their own has come into their life and they have gone forth under the compulsion of that power to break social and economic chains and to preach the gospel to the poor.

Consider our Puritan ancestors. Now when you mention the Puritans some people shrug their shoulders and say offensive words. We admit that they were not perfect. They suffered from the limitations of their times. They had the faults of their virtues. But they loved freedom, and it was out of the womb of Puritanism that the idea of tolerance emerged. Go back, if you doubt my words, to the literature of the early Baptists and independents and Quakers and rediscover what they had to say about liberty of thought and worship and writing and religious organization. From where did they get such ideas? They discovered them because they were people of the Book. They did not understand as we do. They had theories of inspiration that often led them astray. But in spite of their limitations they discovered the liberty of the Christian individual and they made a supremely important contribution to the English character. In fact, out of their efforts and beliefs came the greatest nation of the world.

Or take the great Methodist Revival in England. We admit that the movement was not all that it might have been. But it changed the character of England. The historians tell us that at the beginning of the eighteenth century England was full of ignorance, brutality, drunkenness, gambling, cockfighting, and bullfighting; men were hanged for petty thefts, thrown into foul prisons for their debt, or marched off to fill the ranks of a depleted navy. The historians tell us about the ubiquitous slave trade and how men who deemed themselves Christians took part in it without scruple. At the end of the century England was still not a paradise. But there was a new public conscience. There were voices pleading the sacredness of personality. There were men and women gathering children into schools and bringing decency into prison and freeing the slaves and laying the foundations of self-governing democracies. Why? Because a group of students at Oxford University gathered around the two Testaments and prayed over them until their message burned in their hearts, then they rose up and said, "Woe unto me if I preach not the Gospel of Christ." And everywhere they went they formed groups of serious and joyous men and women who read the Scriptures as thirsty people drink from sparkling springs.

That is why the Bible has been called the textbook of human liberty. Those who believe that the multitudes exist simply to minister to the needs of a pampered few sought to keep this most revolutionary and liberalizing book from the common people. But those who believe that in a Christian society none is pampered and none is crushed, but that all have opportunity to develop whatever God has given them, ought to plead for a Bible in every person's hands.

It is the same with the burning question of peace. War, especially war in modern conditions with all the deadly resources of science, is so insane that any intelligent person might be expected to rise up and say that it is irrational and must somehow be abolished. But the pioneers in the peace movement have not been the intelligentsia, although they are crowding into the ranks now. The pioneers, the ones who prepared the way with years and years of pleading, were religious people who had drawn their inspiration from the Bible and especially from the Gospels. I know that when the history of the abolition of warfare is written, as it will be written sooner or later, else we will perish, will be like the history of the abolition of slavery in this respect, that those who initiated the movement and continued their witness in days of obloquy and persecution, were people who followed the Prince of Peace and who had fed mind and spirit on the Bread of Life.

A New Technique

But what if the Englishman is right? What if the day of books is drawing to a close? Then we must find a new technique. We must get the Bible into the radio. And why not? Why should there not be readings from Jeremiah and Genesis, from the Gospels and the Epistles? Why should there be not only hymns and prayers and sermons and talks but also biblical readings? We must get the Bible into the movies or—as is being done—form a Bible Movie Society. It is necessary to introduce religious pictures into our religious services, combining the reverent with the spectacular. The church has within its grasp—if it has eyes to see and ears to hear—the greatest medium for biblical and spiritual instruction it has ever had.

But the greater necessity is this: that we who are Christians shall be "epistles" who are read and known by others. Even this Englishman anticipates that a minority will cling to their books because they will value and seek to perpetrate the treasures of the past. May we not assume that they will have a commanding influence in a society that is lacking in books and in principles? We must see to it that the message and the spirit of the Bible are perpetrated through us, that others will see in us Abraham who was the friend of God, and Enoch who walked with God, and the Psalmists who sang his praises, and prophets who declared his truth. It won't matter so much if people neglect the sacred page if they can see in us a clear reflection of him of whom Nicodemus said, "We know that thou art a Teacher sent from God." If we are epistles read and known by people, then we may still look forward to liberty and truth, to peace amongst nations, and to a loftier race:

With flame of freedom in their souls,
And light of knowledge in their eyes.[1]

---

[1][From John Addington Symonds (1840–1893), "Hymn" (or "Vista"), a poem later adapted in the early 1900s as "These Things Shall Be," described as a "British labor song."]

For God, through us and through all his chosen people, will still be declaring his Word to all flesh.

The People's Book

There are many subjects that cannot possibly be covered adequately in a single sermon. The Bible is such a subject. To think about it at all is to embark upon vast territories where the possibilities are almost unlimited. I might have shrunk from such a task if I did not believe that the Bible is the greatest book in the world and yet one of the most neglected books in our day. A people that neglect this book will not for long be a free people. They will not be a spiritual people. They will not be an aggressive people. Within this book is God's revelation of himself to humanity. It contains the truth about God and people. It possesses within its pages the secret of inward peace. It tells of the heavenly Father who sent his Son Jesus into our world to redeem us from our sins. Let us think together on the Bible as the people's Book.

Of the making of books there is no end but the majority of them have a very short life. They are like babies that are born with great hopes and expectations but after a few fitful days the heart stops beating and the little body is laid away, mourned by its parents, but otherwise forgotten. There are books that start off with great promise and their names are on everybody's lips, their choicest passages are copied and quoted by many, but in a few years they too perish as though they had not been. Only a few books live through the centuries defying changes of thought and fashion and gathering to themselves in every generation new readers and disciples. Such books in the English language are those of Chaucer and Milton and Bunyan and Shakespeare. These we call the immortals. But even these usually have a limited public. Each of these has his admirers, but only one here and there is translated into many languages, and even then he appeals to a particular type in different races.

Readers of the Book

But the Bible is different; it is the people's Book. You can go back far beyond the Christian era and you will find a man with only a single scroll in his hands. He does not possess the best things in this great Book, yet with sincerity equaled only by enthusiasm he exclaims:

O how I love thy law!
It is my meditation all the day. . . .
Thy Word is a lamp unto my feet,
And a light unto my path. . . .

Thy testimonies have I taken as a heritage for ever;
For they are the rejoicing of my heart.

                              (Psalm 119:97, 105, 111 ASV)

Then later the writings and thoughts of this great man are included in a larger volume that becomes part of the Scriptures of his people. Next we see a youth from Nazareth of Galilee when the labors of the day are over turning to the sacred scrolls to meditate on the sacred Law, the teachings of the Prophets and the songs of the poets of his people. We see him handling the sacred scrolls in the synagogue with reverence and gratitude. About the same time there is another Jewish boy, born and raised in a great Gentile city, sitting at the feet of one of the greatest rabbis of his time and listening to the exposition given of the Scriptures and discussing with fellow students the renderings given. After some years the gracious wisdom of the Man of Galilee and the letters of the man from Tarsus are added to the Book of Books and its influence widens over many peoples.

In my imagination I see a great host of men and women, scholars and farmers, saints and sinners. I see them learning and teaching. I see them toiling day after day and year after year to translate the Bible into English so that we could have in our own language the Word of God. We cannot overstate what we owe to Wycliffe, Tyndale, and Coverdale for their ardent labors in making it possible for us to have God's Word in our own language. I see a girl by the name of Alice Collins in a day when a load of hay would pay for the privilege of reading Wycliffe's Bible for an hour. Bibles were so valuable that they were willed by deed like land and houses and were sold or loaned under seal and witness. I see Alice Collins, who had memorized portions of the Bible, being sent for to recite at large gatherings so those who could not read or were too poor to buy reading time could hear the Word of God.

I see one of the world's greatest statesmen, when the world was seething with tension, sitting in his study reading the wisdom of the ages in a great family Bible. No wonder William Edward Gladstone, in his day, was a leader of people. I see one of the greatest psychologists of our day sitting at his desk writing a book on mental mechanisms, on repression and suggestion, on analysis and sublimation. Before him are many books, books by Jung and Adler and Freud, but also a well-worn copy of the English Bible. Later his book comes from the press and I find it full of biblical illustrations. Naaman the Syrian is there, and Judas Iscariot and Ahab, and Jacob and a dozen more. I say to him, why do you use so many Bible characters and biblical passages in your book? He answers, "I use the biblical material because its psychology is so piercingly true to life and so extraordinarily up to date, and I find a truth and a power that all the writers in my field cannot give."

The Book of Consolation

Now, go with me to the hospital where I often go to visit the sick. Here is an elderly lady who has suffered much from pain and weariness. And she invites me to read to her. Is she asking me to read to her from the latest novel or the daily paper, or a sonnet from Shakespeare or a passage from Wordsworth, or the latest findings of science? No. I ask her, "Where shall I read?" meaning from the Old or the New Testament? And she says, "From the Gospels." "Do you have a special chapter in the Gospels that you wish me to read?" "Yes," she replies, "the ninth of John." So I read to her about the man who was born blind receiving his sight and she stops me at the confident witness of that man to the Pharisees who were trying to confuse him with their cross-examination: "Whether He be a sinner or not, I know not: one thing I know, that, whereas I was blind, now I see." From this passage both the reader and the listener receive fresh food for their souls.

Dr. Ian McLaren tells of an interesting experience he had with William McLure as McClure was coming to the end of this life. McLure said, "I am getting drowsy; read a bit to me." His friend put on his spectacles and began searching for some comforting scriptures. Presently he began to read, "In My Father's house are many mansions"—but McLure stopped him. "It's a good word," he said, "but it is not for the like of me. Shut the book," he said, "and let it open itself." McLaren shut the Book and it opened to the place where Jesus spoke of the pharisee and the publican at prayer. His friend read to him this great story and at the verse, "And the Publican, standing afar-off, would not lift up so much as his eyes to heaven, but smote upon his breast saying, 'God be merciful to me a sinner,' " the dying man exclaimed, "That might have been written for me, or any other old sinner that has finished this life, and has nothing to say for himself."

Fiction, did you say? That sort of thing is happening all over our country, and not our country only, but in England, throughout Europe and in thousands of parts of Asia and Africa. Did you not know that the Bible has been translated into 1,068 different languages and that every six weeks a new translation is completed? Did you not know that people are climbing mountains and making their way through dense forests and jungles in order to circulate the Word and that others are traveling great distances that they may possess them? A few years ago a man walked 85 miles to obtain a latest edition of the Bible. Such people are reading and saying again with the Psalmist: "It is my meditation all the day."

A Hindu teacher said, "I began to study the Bible because someone told me that the best English was found in it. I read it for that purpose, but soon found myself forgetting about the language, for its message gripped me." It was a young Japanese who said, "When I read the Gospels they spoke directly to my soul and I said to myself, 'This is God's Word to me.' " It is the same everywhere and so it will continue to be. Individuals who now speak to their thousands will be forgotten; theories which are accepted as truth will be superceded; but the Bible will still be inspiring the young, strengthening the mature, and comforting the aged.

Why is this? The whole answer cannot be put into a single word or sentence. Much might be said about the Bible's immense range, its variety of mood, for example. It used to be said of a great preacher that everything he said seemed fresh because no one knew what mood he would be in. One day he was all praise and another day all penitence. He would start some service with some such call to worship as, "O, come, let us worship and bow down!" Sometimes he would speak of a God who is almighty and eternal and far beyond human understanding. Again he would speak of a Father God who was the King of Love, who comes very near to people in mercy and forgiveness. The Bible is like that. There are passages for the darkest hours when life is a burden and life's questions are intolerable in their complexity. There are many other passages that are instilled with courage, hope and praise. There are solemn, searching books like Job, Ecclesiastes, and Lamentations and bright buoyant books like the Psalms and Luke's Gospel.

Much more might be said about variety of form. There is poetry for those who appreciate poetry, more of it than is generally realized. There is philosophy for those who appreciate philosophy. There are quiet pastorals like Ruth and strange apocalypses like Daniel. There are plain narratives, moving dramas, and some of the best letters that have ever been written. Do you like books of travel, or proverbial wisdom, or adventures, or love stories, or sermons, or hymns? They are all there in the Bible.

The Book That Searches the Heart

But the Bible is the people's Book most of all because its message is deep enough to touch the profoundest depths of the human soul. Do we not all want to say for ourselves what Coleridge said for himself, "That in the

Bible there is more that finds us than we have experienced in all other books put together; the words of the Bible find us at greater depths of our being"? We read about Cain and his fleshly desires. We read about Jacob with his mixture of craftiness and deep reverence, his willingness to deceive his brother and his ability to wrestle with God till the dawn, and before we have read half there is to read we are reading our own hearts and seeking Esau in our own flesh and Jacob in our own minds. We spend an hour with Absalom the vain prince, with Amos the prophet of righteousness, with Jeremiah and his fount of tears, and with Ruth clinging to Naomi and exclaiming, "Entreat me not to leave thee," and all the time we are discovering new perils and possibilities in our own soul.

And then we come face to face with Jesus, the Prophet, Priest, and King, the Man of Sorrows, the Friend of sinners, the Lover of humankind, the Savior of the world; we come face to face with him as he moves as a man amongst men, as he dies upon a cross, as he rises triumphant over death and sits at the right hand of God, and as we dare to look upon him, heart and mind and soul are flooded with shame and repentance and hope and love and holy resolution. Many questions, no doubt, will lie unanswered in our minds, but our hearts bow before him and with Thomas we say, "My Lord and my God."

Again I say, ought not this Book be in our hands from childhood to old age? Ought it not be the basis of our education? Ought we not show the way to the children that God has given us in our homes and to all men and women who flit from book to book like insects from flower to flower by being the people of the Book? Let us lay to heart its heavenly wisdom and we need envy no one his novels or poems or science.

Part 4

Bible Characters

Elijah, the Son of Thunder

"Behold, Elijah is here."   (1 Kings 18:8)

"Behold, Elijah is here." But what of that? It could be said of a vast number of people and it would mean little or nothing. What difference would it make? The fact that they were here would not rebuke evildoers or encourage those who strive for the truth. It would not help, guide, warn, cheer, comfort, or inspire any soul. But when you say "Behold, Elijah is here" that is a different matter. Let idolaters beware. Let evildoers flee. Let tyrants tremble. Let the discouraged and the disheartened take courage. Let the hopeless have hope. Let all those who have not bowed the knee to Baal rejoice and give thanks. Behold, Elijah is here!

This sentence was spoken under circumstances which, like all the incidents in the life of Elijah, were most dramatic. It was three and a half years after Elijah had pronounced the judgment of the drought upon the idolatrous court and the people, and for three and a half years it had not rained. The whole land languished under the famine. The wicked king Ahab had set out in one direction through the land and his prime minister, Obadiah, who was a God-fearing man, had set out in the other direction to search for water and for pasturage. Obadiah was suddenly confronted by Elijah, who said to him, "Go tell the king, Behold, Elijah is here."

Because of who Elijah was and because of the mighty name in which he spoke, to say "Elijah is here" means that the power of God is present in the lives of people and of nations.

The Comfort and the Kindness of God

To say "Elijah is here" means that we have the comfort and presence of God in the hour of our trial and sorrow. On one occasion our Lord took the disciples apart into a desert place and asked them the world's opinion of him. "Who do men say that I, the Son of Man, am?" They answered that some thought he was the prophet Jeremiah while others were sure that he was another of the great prophets, but some thought that he was Elijah come back to earth. There was indeed much in the life of Elijah, both on his sterner side and on his gentler side, which suggests the life of Christ. On the gentler side we have that similarity to Christ brought out in the story of the widow of Zarephath. It was after Elijah had come from the Brook Cherith in the mountains where he had fled from the wrath of King Ahab after pronouncing the drought upon the land, and where he had been sustained by water out of the brook and by the meat which the ravens brought him every morning and every evening. But after a time the brook dried up, and Elijah was directed to go to the town of Zarephath in Sidon, where he would find a widow who would sustain him. Into that same region our Lord once went, and there he performed one of his most gracious miracles when he healed the only daughter of a poor widow.

When Elijah arrived at the town, he saw this woman gathering sticks to build a fire, and said to her "Fetch me, I pray thee, a little water in a vessel, that I may drink." She went off to get him the drink of water and Elijah called after her and said, "Bring me I pray thee a morsel of bread in thine hand." At that, the woman threw up her hands in a gesture of despair and exclaimed, "As the Lord thy God liveth, I have not a cake, but a handful of meal in a barrel, and a little oil in a cruse; and behold, I am gathering two sticks, that I may go in and dress it for me and my son that we may eat it and die." But Elijah said to her, "Fear not . . . make me of it a little cake first, and bring it unto me, and afterwards make for thee and for thy son. . . . The barrel of meal shall not waste, neither shall the cruse of oil fail." And that was exactly what happened.

In all the ages since the phrase "the widow's barrel of meal and the widow's cruse of oil" has stood for the providence of God and his care in our lives. Elijah is here. Underneath and about us are the everlasting arms. Therefore be of good courage.

The Judgments of God and Divine Retribution

When we say "Elijah is here" it also means that the judgments and justice of God are at work in the world. The entire career of Elijah and the judgments that he pronounced upon the wicked court and the apostate nation reveal this important and impressive truth: God's eyes are on the wicked and they shall not go unpunished.

True religion and morality had almost disappeared in the land of Israel. Under the domination of his wicked and idolatrous wife, Jezebel, Ahab had sunk the nation in sin. The bull god of Baal was set up all over the land and the worshippers of the Lord were proscribed and persecuted. It was in view of that fact that God sent Elijah to pronounce his judgments. The announcement of Obadiah to Ahab that "Elijah is here" was equivalent to saying "Elijah is here; therefore you and your false prophets of Baal had better tremble."

In view of what is going on in the world today, it is a mighty reinforcement to our faith and courage to remember that Elijah is here; that is, that God has not forsaken the world, that he has not forsaken his people and that he beholds the injustice and iniquity which are done on the earth. Payday is sure to come for those people and nations that wax mighty in the way of evil. Let us be sure that we are pursuing the course of life that is honoring and well pleasing to God.

Not only did the presence of Elijah mean a judgment upon the entire nation but also upon Ahab in particular for an act of great wickedness and cruelty. One evening while taking a stroll, Ahab came upon a vineyard the location and the cultivated fruitful state of which, with its well-kept tower and fruitful vines, struck him as making a property greatly to be desired—all the more so because it was near his palace in Jezreel. Ahab inquired of some officers as to the identity of the owner, and when he learned that it was Naboth, he sent him a proposal, offering a sum of money for the vineyard or, if he preferred, he would buy him another vineyard. But to his astonishment Naboth declined the offer. The king probably offered him twice as much the second time but still Naboth refused to sell. He said that it had been in his family for generations and he would not part with it for any sum of money. It is always refreshing to find a person like that whether he lives in the days of Elijah or in the present time. Neither Naboth nor his vineyard was for sale.

That night the disappointed Ahab came to his palace heavy and displeased, and like a spoiled child would not sit down to his dinner, but lay down on his bed and turned his face to the wall. Queen Jezebel, the real force around that palace and the Lady Macbeth of the Old Testament, came into the king and asked him, "What is the trouble? Why are you lying there on the bed with that dismal expression on your face? Why don't you get up and eat your dinner?" Ahab then related to her the incident of the vineyard and how Naboth refused to sell it. When she heard the story, Jezebel said, "What kind of king are you anyway? Get up and eat your dinner, and be merry in heart, and leave Naboth's vineyard to me." Then the wicked queen wrote letters to her officers and sealed them with the seal of Ahab. In the letters she gave directions to the officers of the city to have Naboth arrested and charged with blasphemy by false witnesses. This was done. The innocent, high-minded and courageous Naboth was brought to trial and convicted of blasphemy against God. The punishment was death by stoning. The stoning took place near the pool of Samaria where the harlots bathed.

After Naboth had been stoned to death, the scavenger dogs gathered round and greedily licked up the blood that flowed from his mangled body.

Then word was sent to Jezebel that Naboth was dead, and Jezebel told the king to go down and possess the vineyard "For," said she, "Naboth is not alive, but dead." Yes, Naboth was dead but God was not dead, retribution was not dead and Elijah was not dead. The king in great delight went down to possess the vineyard but he had hardly entered the gates of the vineyard and had not yet tasted of the first of its ripe grapes when he was confronted by none other than Elijah. Behold, Elijah is here. When Ahab saw the prophet of God, he exclaimed "Hast thou found me, O mine enemy?" Elijah answered "I have found thee." Elijah was Ahab's conscience. Conscience cannot be stoned to death. Conscience cannot be bribed. Conscience cannot be killed. To every doer of evil conscience will eventually say "I have found thee."

Elijah, standing before the guilty king, prophesied Ahab's death and also this incident in connection with his death: "Where the dogs licked the blood of Naboth shall dogs lick thy blood, even thine." After that Ahab had no delight in the vineyard. Whenever he went out to walk in the evening, he was sure to pass it by, for he could hear the blood of Naboth calling from the earth for vengeance; and wherever he went, there followed the awful echo of Elijah's words "Where the dogs lick thy blood, even thine."

But the weeks and the months and the years passed and nothing happened. Ahab no doubt thought that the judgment pronounced upon him by Elijah had misfired. But one day he went up to battle with Jehoshaphat, the king of Judah, against the Syrian stronghold, Ramoth-Gilead. As the chariots were rolling to and fro, and the armies were maneuvering for the onset of the battle, Ahab remembered Elijah's melancholy prediction, and taking off his royal robes, disguised himself as a private soldier. Thus he hoped to escape vengeance and death in the battle. But a certain man, one of those anointed agents of divine retribution, drew his bow at a venture, not aiming at any one in particular. But the arrow was aimed by the hand of God. It smote Ahab in the joints of his harness and inflicted a mortal wound. The king courageously stayed himself up in the chariot until the sun was set, when he died. Then, in the retreat of his army his chariot with his dead body in it was driven back to Jezebel. The charioteer drove the bloody chariot down to the pool of Samaria to wash out the blood that had flowed from the king's wounds and as he did so, the dogs, the very dogs that there had licked the blood of Naboth, gathered round and licked up the blood of Ahab from the floor of the chariot.

Elijah is here. Let evildoers and tyrants tremble.

Czechoslovakia is crushed. Poland is a shambles and a waste. Greece is fallen. Manila is possessed by the enemy. Nevertheless, let the tyrants and dictators beware. Elijah is here. God has not abdicated his throne. There is a law of retribution and of justice which works among people and nations and which will not fail of its vengeance.

The Power of Prayer

When we say "Elijah is here" it means that we have the power and the help of prayer. James adds to our knowledge of Elijah and the great judgment of the drought that fell upon the land. In the story in the Book of Kings we are told merely that Elijah predicted the drought (1 Kings 17:1), but James says that this judgment came in answer to the prayer of Elijah. James says: "Elias was a man subject to like passions as we are, and he prayed earnestly that it might not rain: and it rained not on the earth by the space of three years and six months. And he prayed again, and the heaven gave rain, and the earth brought forth her fruit" (James 5:17-18). James says this in connection with his statement that "the effectual fervent prayer of a righteous man availeth much" (James 5:16).

All the great events in the life of Elijah show the power of prayer and how effectual the prayer of a godly person is. Elijah prayed that it might not rain and it rained not on the earth for three and a half years. He prayed again and there was rain on the earth. Dramatic too is the story of how Elijah relied upon prayer in his battle with the priests of Baal. He had challenged them and the entire nation to a trial by fire. After the priests of Baal had leaped and danced and cut themselves with stones and prayed in vain to Baal to send down fire and consume the offerings, Elijah built his altar and drenched the offering with water and then offered his heartfelt prayer: "Hear me, O Lord, hear me, that this people may know that thou art the Lord God, and that thou hast turned their heart back again" (1 Kings 18:37).When he had so prayed the fire fell down from heaven and consumed the burnt offering and the water that filled the trenches.

Then Elijah announced to Ahab that the rain was coming. He sent his servant to the top of Carmel while he himself cast himself on the ground and with his head between his knees called upon God. The servant stood on the top of Carmel and looking off over the Mediterranean saw not a sign of rain. The sky was like brass and the sea like glass without a ruffle on its surface. When he went back to his master Elijah he said, "There is nothing." Elijah told him to go and look again, and again he went to the top of

Carmel, while Elijah lay on the ground with his head between his knees. Again the young man returned to Elijah and said, "There is nothing." And the prophet told him to go again. He went again the third time, and the fourth time, and the fifth time, and the sixth time, and every time he reported, "There is nothing." But Elijah told him to go the seventh time and that time when he looked, behold, a cloud was on the horizon no larger than a man's hand. Soon there was the rush of the wind and the sound of the abundance of rain and Elijah girding up his loins ran in triumph before Ahab to his palace at Jezebel.

Behold, Elijah is here. When you pray, remember Elijah.

The Certainty and the Glory of the Life to Come

When we say "Elijah is here" it means that we live after death and that that life is one of power and glory. There was grandeur and pathos too about the translation of Elijah and the end of his earthly life. A lonely man all his days, Elijah wanted to be alone when the end came. But the faithful Elisha would not leave him. Together therefore they went down to the Jordan, where Elijah took his mantle and smote the waters and together they went over the river. Then as they talked together a chariot of fire and horses of fire parted them and Elijah went up in a whirlwind into heaven.

That sublime ending to Elijah's earthly life was in itself a magnificent testimony to the truth that good people never die, that death cannot conquer them, and that they have their exceeding great reward. But in the history of Elijah as it is completed by the inspired penmen of the New Testament we have something even greater than that sublime scene by the Jordan when Elijah went up into heaven in a whirlwind.

With Peter and James and John, Jesus climbed to the top of the mountain and there, while the disciples slept and as he prayed, Jesus was transfigured before them and his countenance was bright with the glory of heaven. When the disciples awoke, to their amazement they saw Moses and Elijah standing by the side of Jesus and conversing with him. How exciting must have been their exclamation as Peter said to James and James said to John, "Behold, Elijah is here."

The appearance of Elijah in glory by the side of our Lord on the Mount of Transfiguration declares the fact of the glory of our life after death. Elijah is not merely a great memory, he is not the citizen of a sepulcher, he is not a handful of dust blown about the Syrian hills, but he is rather a living man, a living soul, for God is not the God of the dead, but of the living.

Elijah, with all the power of his mind, appears in the fellowship of Moses and of Christ and converses with them about the great fact of all the ages.

And what was that fact? What was the theme and subject of Elijah and Moses when they talked with Christ? It was the subject upon which God himself first spoke when he said to the man and the woman after the fall that the seed of the woman should bruise the head of the serpent. It was the fact of which God spoke to Abraham when he told him to offer up Isaac on Mount Moriah and told him that because of his obedience in him all the nations of the earth would be blessed. It was the subject of which Balaam sang when he said, "There shall come a star out of Jacob, and a scepter shall rise out of Israel." It was the subject of which God spoke to Moses when he gave him instruction for the altars of sacrifice and the Day of Atonement, the subject of which David sang when he spoke of Christ and his kingdom, the subject of which Jeremiah spoke when he said that the day would come when God would make a New Covenant with his people, the subject of which Isaiah spoke when he painted his great picture of the One who was despised and rejected of men, the Man of Sorrows and acquainted with grief the subject of which Peter spoke when he said that we have been redeemed not with corruptible things, but with the precious blood of Christ, as a Lamb without spot and blemish, the subject in which Paul gloried when he said "God forbid that I should glory, save in the cross of our Lord Jesus Christ," the subject which John on his isle of exile said was the great theme and the great music of the New Jerusalem, when he saw the multitude that had come out of great tribulation and washed their robes and made them white in the blood of the Lamb.

And what subject is this? It is the power of God unto salvation, the power of the cross to save from sin. That was what Elijah and Moses talked with Christ about—the majesty of it, the sublimity of it, and the ineffable glory of it.

Through your faith in Jesus Christ, through your fidelity to God, will the angels of heaven be able to say to God, substituting your name for the name of Elijah "Behold he is here"?

The Riddle of Life

Out of the eater came forth meat, and out of the strong came forth sweetness.   (Judges 14:14)

The wife of Manoah bore a son and called his name Samson, and according to the word of the angel, dedicated him to God from the day of his birth. When he was grown to young manhood he fell in love. His choice was not altogether fortunate. A marriage with one of the hereditary enemies of Israel was repugnant and distasteful to Manoah and his wife. Manoah stormed and his wife wept but Samson would not be moved. "Get her for me" he said, "for I love her well." Reluctantly, they gave their consent. And Samson, greatly elated, went down for an interview with this Philistine beauty. On the way down a young lion leaped out of the brush and roared against him, but Samson seized the lion and rent it in twain, as he would rend a kid.

Arrangements were made for the wedding and Samson with his father and mother were again on the way to Timnath. Leaving the path he turned aside to see what had become of the lion that he had slain on the previous trip. Vultures and ants had stripped the bones clean of the flesh, but in the ribs of the lion the bees had hived. Samson took his fill of the sweet honey and gave a portion to his father and mother, not telling them, however, of his dangerous encounter with the lion.

It was a custom to propound riddles at the bridegroom's banquet. This huge bridegroom now put forth his riddle. If within seven days they could answer him, he would give them thirty shirts and thirty changes of garments. Thus the odds were thirty to one and yet Samson was not taking chances because no one would have ever guessed such a riddle as he propounded. It was this: "Out of the eater came forth meat, and out of the strong came forth sweetness."

For several days the Philistines wrestled with this enigma. Unable to solve it, they went to the bride and demanded that she get from Samson the answer to his riddle. If she did not, they would burn her and her father's house. The frightened woman begged him to tell her the secret. When Samson refused, she reproached him. Here was a battle in which Samson had no experience. Samson stood the bombardment for seven days and then succumbed and told his wife what she wanted to know. She at once informed the thirty banqueters and before the sun went down on the seventh day they came to him and said: "What is sweeter than honey? And what is stronger than a lion?"

Samson, suspicious now as to how they had guessed it, retorted, "If ye had not plowed with my heifer, ye had not guessed my riddle" (Judges 14:18).

This riddle we lift out of its immediate setting and take for the statement of the great truth that out of temptation met and conquered comes strength and influence and happiness and out of struggle, trial, suffering, and sorrow come those virtues which adorn and strengthen human life. "Out of the eater came forth meat, and out of the strong came forth sweetness."

Temptation

This is no Seven Days' Battle or Thirty Years' War, but rather the normal warfare appointed unto humanity. Temptation is as universal as human nature and as eternal as human history. Standing in the illuminated passages of some of the great limestone caverns, one can hear, when voices are silent, the murmur of a subterranean river flowing silently away. So through human life flows the river of temptation. Man's history begins with an encounter with temptation. When Samson the young man went down to Timnath a young lion roared against him. So temptation, no matter what the path the young man takes, is sure to assail him. On every path of life you can hear the soul-seeking roar of that lion of temptation.

Out of the encounter with temptation and the opposition to it comes strength of character. What is the difference between the soft face of a child and the face of man? One has been tried on the battlefield of life and the other has not. There is no such thing as artificial, made-to-order morality. Moral character must be won on the battlefield. Christ told James and John that to sit at his right hand or at his left was not his to give, but that such honors would be bestowed upon those who won them by drinking his cup and going down into his baptism. Courage is won in the face of danger, truth under the temptation of falsehood, calmness in the resistance to danger, and purity through the repulse of the tempted. "In your patience," said Christ—literally in your "sufferings"—"ye shall possess your souls" (Luke 21:19).

There is no joy like that of overcoming temptation. With great satisfaction, Samson tasted of the sweet honey which had been deposited in the ribs of the beast he had slain. Temptation conquered is honey far sweeter than that dropped from the honeycomb. There is always a pleasant sensation in the recollection of that which we have won by our struggles. But sweetest of all is the recollection of victory won over temptation and sin. The honey and sweetness of surrender to temptation, while lasting for a moment, soon turns to bitterness and gall. The evangelists tell us that when Jesus had overcome his temptation the angels came and ministered unto him. That is an eternal and beautiful parable of the truth that angels of satisfaction and joy come to visit us when we have said to Satan "Get thee behind me" and have chosen truth rather than falsehood, suffering rather than dishonor, and the rights of the soul rather than the appetites of the body.

Out of Adversity and Trial
Come the Virtues of a Christian Life

Virtues such as patience, courage, kindness, sympathy, power, and influence are won out of the struggles of life. This is true first of all as to accomplishment and success in the world. We have heard it said of certain people that they had too much money when they were young. This is given as an explanation of their uselessness and failure. But you never heard it said, by way of explaining someone's ill success, "He had no money." Why is this? Because we all recognize that an environment of denial, privation, and struggle has a tendency to evoke the latent talents of the soul. Professor Conklin writes:

> What is needed in education more than anything else is some means or system which will train the powers of self-discovery and self-control. Easy lives and so-called "good environment" will not arouse the dormant powers. It usually takes the stress and the strain of hard necessity to make us acquainted with our hidden selves, to rouse the sleeping giant within us. How often it is said that worthless sons of worthy parents are mysteries; with the best of heredity and environment they amount to nothing, whereas the sons of poor and ignorant farmers, blacksmiths, tanners, and backwoodsmen, with few opportunities and with many hardships and disadvantages, become world figures. Probably the inheritance in these last-named cases named was no better than the former, but the environment was better.[1]

---

[1][Edwin Grant Conklin, *Heredity and Environment in the Development of Men*, 5th ed. rev. (Princeton NJ: Princeton University Press; London: Oxford University Press, 1922; [1]1915) 335.]

What is true of success in the world, that hardship and trial are incentives that help to such success, is true of that higher and invisible success which is more important than all, the success and standing of our souls in things spiritual and moral. Hezekiah, after his sore sickness, in his song of thanksgiving, the meaning of adversity made clear to him, said, "By these things men live" (Isaiah 38:16). David, after his trials, said, "It is for my good that I was afflicted" (Psalm 119:71). And what a story the tale of Joseph is of strength and honor and power coming to the man who had put temptation under his feet and had passed through tribulation. At the end of it all he was able to say to his brethren who mistakenly imagined that he was going to take vengeance upon them, "As for you, ye meant evil against me, but God meant it for good" (Genesis 50:20). Yes, and not only Joseph can say that. How many others can rise up and testify to the meat that came out of the eater and to the sweetness that came out of the carcass of the lion, and how what threatened to engulf, overwhelm, and destroy, brought to them their deepest convictions, their most powerful thoughts and their most abiding satisfactions?

The medieval theologians used to discuss the question as to whether or not thistles grew in Paradise. Some said no. Others said yes, but that the thistles had no power to hurt humanity in its unfallen state. This is one way of expressing the truth that the thorns and adversities of life cannot really hurt the believing and trustful soul and that all things work together for good to them that love God.

Conclusion

The Riddle of the Universe, Ernst Haeckel called his celebrated book in which he so glibly dispensed with God, the soul, and immortality.[2] But that is a poor way of solving the riddle. Life has many facts, many happenings, which taken by themselves are inexplicable, baffling, perplexing, and even overwhelming. They raise great questions as to the value of life and as to the realities of the spiritual world. "Where is now thy God?" The riddle that solves the riddle of life is this truth which has been suggested by the hero of ancient Israel, that out of the eater comes forth meat, and out of the strong sweetness. In other words, the great end and purpose of life is moral

---

[2][Ernst Heinrich Phillipp August Haeckel, *The Riddle of the Universe at the Close of the Nineteenth Century*, trans. Joseph McCabe (New York, London: Harper & Brothers, 1900).]

and probationary; all those experiences through which we are called upon to pass serve the purpose of developing those moral powers that will lead us successfully into the world to come.

No sound Christian view of life will leave out either of these facts: first, that the experiences of life can produce virtue; and second, that this life must be related to the life that is to come. Therefore, relate your life to its great goal and purpose. Make your plans not for twenty-four hours, but for eternity. Base your convictions and draw your deductions not from a single experience, or a single life, but from the connection which the experiences of this life have with the life which is to come.

On a Virginia monument I saw some time ago was a tribute to some soldiers that had died in battle. The inscription ended with this fine sentence: "They teach us how to suffer and grow strong." "Out of the strong came forth sweetness, and out of the eater came forth meat."

The high and beautiful illustration of this is the cross of Calvary. Christ before he died said, "Except a corn of wheat fall into the ground and die, it abideth alone" (John 12:24). What a profound and wonderful expression of the spiritual reach and power of his own life. Out of the darkness and night and cries and anguish of Calvary comes the great victory over death and hell. The thorns of Calvary which were pressed upon his brow now bloom for us; they blossom for us into the flowers of Paradise. The Cross is the solution to the riddle of life. To all life's longings, cries, disappointments, anguish of soul and body, to that strange, strange riddle, the answer is the eternal Cross, where death brought forth life, where the wrath of humanity brought forth love, and where sin and guilt flowered into peace and forgiveness.

I Go a-Fishing

Simon Peter saith unto them, "I go a-fishing."   (John 21:3)

It is hard for ministers of the Gospel to make up their minds whether to put a favorable or an unfavorable interpretation upon these words. What did Peter mean when he said to his companions, "I go a-fishing"? Did he mean "While we are waiting for Jesus let us go on with our every day duties"? Or did he mean "It is of no use waiting any longer. I am going back to my old job"? Was Peter simply intent on earning his own living until Jesus came to give him orders or was he on the point of deserting altogether? I find it very difficult to decide, for there is much to be said in support of both views. I propose to give you both interpretations and allow you to choose for yourselves.

Let me begin with the circumstances involved. The story is a story of the days after our Lord's resurrection. I am not sure that it is possible to make an absolutely clear and consecutive story of what happened in the forty days that intervened between the resurrection and the ascension. The first appearances of the risen Christ took place in Jerusalem. We are told that on Easter Day he appeared to Mary, to Peter, to the two disciples on the way to Emmaus, and then to the whole body of disciples gathered in the Upper Room. Then we hear of no further appearance until a week later, when again Jesus appeared to the disciples in the Upper Room for the special benefit of Thomas.

It appears that after the second Sunday the apostles had returned to Galilee. We must never forget that the apostles were Galileans and that their homes were there. I suppose for example that Peter, even during those years he was in close contact with Jesus, kept his home in Bethsaida. It was quite natural therefore that the apostles should leave Jerusalem, which they were visiting for the Passover season, for their native province, especially since they had been told by an angel that Jesus would meet them in Galilee.

So I imagine them setting their faces homeward with the great hope of meeting their Lord again and perhaps resuming the happy relationship of previous days. But day after day passed and brought no sign of Jesus. A group of seven disciples led by Peter seem to have clung together waiting for Jesus' reappearance. But nothing happened. No Jesus came. Every day ended in disappointment. And at last, one day Peter broke out with "I go a-fishing." And the others promptly replied, "We also go with thee." Now, what are we to make of this? Is it a word of despair? Does Peter say in effect, "It is of no use waiting any longer, I am going back to my old job"?

The Unfavorable Verdict

There are many things to suggest such an interpretation. There is first of all the character of Peter himself. He was an impetuous, impulsive and unreliable person. Peter was subject to great gusts of enthusiasm. But people who quickly kindle into enthusiasm easily fall into depression. Great exaltations are often followed by deep dejections. It would not surprise me to find Peter, who was so overjoyed with the appearance of his Lord on Easter Day, falling into despair of ever seeing Jesus again when the days passed and Jesus did not return.

In the second place, Peter was a fisherman. And those whose business lies in the great waters never lose their love for their craft. Peter had left his boat and his nets when he followed Jesus but the boats and nets were still there. So when Peter returned to Bethsaida and saw his boats and his nets, felt the smell of the lake in his nostrils, and thought of the quiet nights beneath the stars and the excitement of pulling in the nets, all the love of his old craft swept over him and he said, "I go a-fishing." He was going back to his old business; he was giving up all ideas of catching people to return to the humbler task of catching fish. Peter at that moment was in danger of deserting the cause of Christ.

I am more disposed to accept this interpretation of Peter's action because of the question Jesus put to him after breakfast. "Simon, son of John," Jesus said to him, "lovest thou me more than these?" Jesus did not mean more than these other disciples, more than James and John and Thomas and Philip. I cannot bring myself to believe that Jesus would make such a comparison. I cannot imagine Jesus saying to Peter, "Lovest thou me more than John?" When Jesus said to Peter, "Lovest thou me more than these?" he was speaking of the boats and nets and fishing gear, those things by which Peter in the old days had earned his livelihood and to which now he was inclined to return. I believe that by this question Jesus was reminding Peter that unless he was prepared to leave all and follow him he could not be his disciple. These considerations move me to think that Peter was in danger of deserting Jesus for his former trade and of imitating those Galileans who went back and walked no more with him.

In the epistle that bears his name Peter dealt with some impatient folk who said, "Where is the promise of his coming?" and who were inclined to give up their faith because of Christ's delay in coming again. He himself had been in the very same peril when he said, "I go a-fishing" because he had been inclined to go back to his old business and back to the world that he had left, all because he thought Jesus had either forgotten or neglected his promise.

But if Peter at this juncture was inclined to turn his back upon Jesus, Jesus had no intention of letting him go. There was an amazing persistence in our Lord's love for this impulsive and warmhearted but unstable man. "Simon, Simon," he said to him one day, "behold, Satan hath desired to have you, that he may sift you as wheat; but I have prayed for thee that thy faith fail not" (Luke 22:31-32). There was a tussle between Satan and Jesus for the soul of Peter. There was an old Jewish legend that Michael and Satan wrestled for the body of Moses. No, I don't think Satan wrestles over dead bodies: what Satan wrestles for is souls. It is not with any archangel he wrestles but with Jesus himself. And Satan would have captured the soul of Peter had it not been for Jesus. "I have prayed for thee that thy faith fail not." Satan came near to claiming Peter when in the Judgment Hall Peter cursed and swore, saying that he did not even know Jesus. Satan really thought Peter was his that day. But the Lord turned and looked upon Peter—and that look broke his heart. And on the morning of the third day he sent a special message of love to Peter—and that message saved his soul.

Satan did not take that defeat as final, though. He returned again to the charge, this time through the appeal of boats and nets and the sea. It looked almost as if he had won when Peter said to the other disciples, "I go a-fishing." But Jesus was watching over this dear but unstable disciple of his. Peter and his companions caught nothing that night. I believe their bad fishing luck was Jesus' way of telling them that fishing was not to be their business in life. And in the morning there he was upon the shore. The vision of the Lord put Satan to flight. "Lord," said Peter, "thou knowest all things; thou knowest that I love thee" (John 21:17). It was the persistent love of Jesus that saved Peter. He could anticipate George Matheson and say, "O love that wilt not let me go."

Now, what are the lessons for us from this interpretation? Christian people from the very first have been tempted to give up their faith because of the Lord's delays. There are times in our experiences when Jesus is very near to us and very real. In such days we are ready to forsake all and follow him. He is to us the pearl of great price for which we are ready to sell all that we have. But there are other days when we miss him, when he becomes far off and unreal. And in those days we are sorely tempted to go back to our old ways, back to what corresponds in our case to Peter's boats and nets and fishing gear, back to the lust of the eye and the lust of the flesh and the vainglory of life. The danger to our religious life comes in the dull drab days when Jesus does not appear. It comes in the reaction, for example, that often follows days of spiritual exaltation and revival, the days when nothing happens, when no glory gilds the skies, when no warmth suffuses the heart, when we are tempted to ask "Is Jesus real?" and "Is religion worthwhile?" We are in the mood in times like those to say, like Peter, "I go a-fishing. I am going back to the old life: there was at any rate some thrill and excitement in that." And we too might fall victim to Satan's wiles, and we too might make our bed in hell, were it not that Jesus is watching us, and that Jesus is pursuing us with his love—that love will not let us go.

Days come to the church when it is in peril of losing faith and hope—those days when there are no visible signs of his presence and his activity, days when we toil all night and catch nothing, days when we are temped to despair and to wonder whether there is really anything in our religion at all. Perhaps we are passing through such a time just now. There is a great decay of faith. There is a widespread revival of paganism. People are neglecting the spiritual and the eternal and saying, "I am going a-fishing. I am going to get all I can out of this world." It is a hard time for us. But Jesus is watching all the time. He is even now giving us signs and proofs of his presence. When night breaks for us we shall find Jesus on the shore and when he bids us let down our nets for a draught we shall not be able to draw the net for the multitude of fishes.

The Favorable Verdict

Now let me pass from the unfavorable view of this word of Peter's to the more favorable view, which the majority of commentators take. When Peter said, "I go a-fishing," the commentators tell us, there was no suggestion of desertion or of abandoning the Christian cause. Peter was not suggesting that he and the other apostles should go back to their old job; rather he was reminding his fellow disciples that during these days of waiting there were certain everyday duties that had to be performed. Waiting need not be synonymous with idleness. They could discharge the prosaic duty of earning a livelihood for themselves and their families. Duty has to be done on the drab days. When the vision fails there are certain plain obligations to be filled. "I go a-fishing," said Peter, as if to say, "Even if Jesus does not come, there is a plain immediate duty that needs to be done."

This view of Peter's word contains a lesson for us all. There come days to us when Jesus seems far off and unreal and remote. You remember the heart cry in that familiar hymn, "Where is the blessedness that I knew when first I saw the Lord?" William Cowper was bewailing the absence of Jesus when he wrote these lines. There come times to us all when we can echo Cowper's words. In fact, great and exalted experiences, those times in which we become vividly aware of Christ, when we are carried away into the third heaven because Christ is so blessedly near, only occur now and then—just sufficiently often to make us absolutely sure of him. The great majority of our days are not marked by sudden splendors of that sort. We are not caught up into paradise and we have just to trudge the common and dusty ways of life. But even on common days there are certain duties to be done. There are obligations to be fulfilled.

There are several parables in the New Testament that speak about servants and their absent Lord. Of course, the happiness of the household is only complete when the master returns, but no one knows when that return will be. But in the meantime, the servants have their duties to fulfill—the porter to guard the door and keep the house in safety, the steward to give all the servants their portion of meat in due season, and so on. And the best way of watching and waiting for the coming of the Lord is faithfully to discharge the humble daily duty. "Blessed is that servant, whom his Lord when he cometh, shall find so doing" (Matthew 24:46). There are simple religious duties we can fulfill even though we experience no overriding sense of the Lord's presence. We can assemble ourselves for worship, we can read our Bibles, and we can pray. We can faithfully observe these religious practices even though worship and scripture and prayer may seem to leave our souls still parched and dry.

Even though Jesus himself seems far away, he has left us with his example. He has revealed to us his will. And we can carry out that will. We can be kind and loving and helpful even on the dull and drab days of life. And that is the real test of our devotion to Christ, that we faithfully and loyally do his will even when we miss his presence. That was what Simon Peter did. "I go a-fishing," he said. There was no great joy for him, for his Lord was absent, but there was work to do and he did it.

There are some who miss Christ in a more tragic way. They lose him in the fogs and mists of doubt. But even when Christ is lost certain obligations and duties, such as honor and truth and kindness, remain. That is exactly how F. W. Robertson felt. After years in the ministry doubts came sweeping down upon him, so that for a time he felt compelled to give up his ministry and to cease from preaching. They were dark hours and weeks, those weeks of stress and storms when he lost his hold of Christ. But in the darkest hour there were some things he was quite sure about, simple and elementary though they were. He was quite sure it was better to be true than false, better to be generous than mean, better to be kind than selfish, better to be pure than impure, better to be good than bad. To those convictions Robertson held. It was a terrible time. Christ was absent but there were plain obligations to be fulfilled.[1]

So certain things remain obligatory even if Jesus for the moment be lost. The landmarks of morality remain. Duty remains. Honor, truth, kindness—these remain binding obligations still. At such a time as that a person must be faithful however hard it is. He must believe that it is better to play the human being than to play the beast. Even when Jesus is lost a person can say with Peter, "I go a-fishing," and do the plain and obvious and immediate duty.

The Reward of Faithfulness

Taking this favorable view of Peter's remark, the story suggests that the faithful discharge of duty is the way to a restored fellowship. I wonder whether Jesus would have appeared to these disciples if they had spent their time restlessly watching for his appearance. But Peter said, "I go a-fishing: there is a duty to be done and I am going to do it," and the rest responded, "We also go with thee." As a result, these seven men, patiently and faithfully doing their appointed tasks, in the morning found Jesus waiting for them on the shore.

There is nothing surprising in all this. It is in line with the teaching of the Bible from beginning to end. God constantly revealed himself to people who were trudging along the ways of simple duty. Here is a sentence about one of the patriarchs: "And Jacob went on his way, and the angels of God met him" (Genesis 32:1). The way Jacob went was not exactly a pleasant way. Jacob trembled as he took it, for out there somewhere was Esau with his 400 men. But it was the way of duty and Jacob took it, even though with a fearful heart, and as Jacob went on his way, the angels of God met him. As he followed the path of duty he got the assurance of the divine presence and protection.

---

[1][Frederick William Robertson (1816–1853), a much-respected English (Anglican) pastor and preacher, known as "Robertson of Brighton" (after his famous ministry at Trinity Chapel, Brighton, 1847 until his untimely death).]

Here is a sentence from the New Testament: "As they went, they were healed." As they obeyed the command of Jesus the blessing came. Jesus himself told us in so many words that the way to gain the blessed sense of his presence is faithfully to do his will. Listen to what I sometimes think is the most amazing promise in the whole Bible: "If a man love me, he will keep my words; and my Father will love him, and we will come unto him, and make our abode with him" (John 14:23). To make sure that Christ will come, we must keep his words. So if at the moment worship seems profitless and the heavens are as brass to our prayers, and if even the Scriptures seem void of spirit and life, let us continue to worship and read and pray, and soon we shall find the dear Lord at our side.

If it is dark night with us because for the moment we have lost him in the fogs of doubt, let us do our plain duty and practice the things we know—let us keep truth and do justice, let us live lives of loving helpfulness—and before long we shall recover our vision of the Lord. So it was with Robertson and so it has been with all who have faithfully discharged their duty. Their night passed and they emerged into a glad and sunny day.

It may be that at the moment we feel that Jesus is far away from us. And because he is far away our religion is sapless and our very life lacks zest and joy for it is only when Jesus is present that there is fullness of joy in any life. Well, how are we to get Jesus back? How are we again to experience the joy of his presence? Not by scanning the heavens. Not by sighing, "Return, O holy Dove, return." Jesus will return to us when we humbly and faithfully do his will as he has revealed it to us. When we are ready with Peter to say, "I go a-fishing," we may have a dark night to pass through. We may, like Peter, toil all the night and catch nothing, but in the morning we shall see Jesus on the shore.

Part 5

Evangelism and Missions

The Missionary Call
of the Old Testament

Now the word of the Lord came unto Jonah. . . . Arise, go to Nineveh, that great city, and cry against it. . . . So Jonah arose, and went unto Nineveh. . . . So the people of Nineveh believed God.
(Jonah 1:1, 2; 3:3, 5 KJV)

I am concerned this morning about the motive behind our mission work. If our motive is right then we need to have no fear regarding it. It is for this reason that I have chosen this Old Testament legend or narrative for our study.

George Adam Smith said in his commentary on the prophet Jonah:

> This is the tragedy of the Book of Jonah, that a book which is made the means of one of the most sublime revelations of truth in the Old Testament should be known to most only for its connection with a whale.[1]

Yes, that is the tragedy. Many a passage, many a book in the Bible, has suffered sorely at the hands of good Christian people. They have been treated as armories of proof texts without any reference to the main lines of the writers' thought. Books like the Book of Daniel and the Book of Revelation are persistently abused by a whole school of Christian people who scan them only to discover in them what they imagine to be "signs of the times" without troubling themselves in the slightest about the meaning of Jewish Apocalyptic and without worrying about the historical situation out of which the authors wrote. Judging from the way in which some people handle these books you might imagine that the authors were not writing for their own age at all, but that all the while they had modern times in mind.

But while many books in the Bible have been mishandled and abused, no book has suffered such outrage as this book of the prophet Jonah. All the attention has been concentrated on the story of the whale as if that were the central thing in the book. Nine out of ten Christian people know it only for that and would be hard put to give any account of the book except that it

---

[1][George Adam Smith, *The Book of the Twelve Prophets*, 2 vols., rev. ed. (New York: Harper & Bros., 1928; Garden City NY: Doubleday, Doran, 1929) 2:492.]

contains that story. It might be a sort of Old Testament Jules Verne story, a Jewish anticipation of the Tarzan series. We don't trouble our heads about the accuracy or veracity of these modern books. They are confessedly books of the imagination and we accept them as such. But this book which contains the whale story is in the Bible and that makes a world of difference. People have debated and discussed and wrangled and quarreled as to the interpretation to be put upon this story. Literalists have contended that it is just sober matter of fact and have devoted much ingenuity to the task of proving its possibility. Frank Bullen wrote a whole chapter in one of his whaling narratives to prove that a whale could really swallow a man. Belief in the story became a test of orthodoxy, a test even of genuine Christianity. And in the dust raised about the story, the real meaning and purpose of the book were entirely overlooked. The result of all this again has been that to the average person the book has become a joke and a jest.

That is the sheer tragedy for this book of Jonah is one of the noblest in the whole of the Old Testament. Of all Old Testament books it is the one that comes nearest in spirit to the New Testament. In its wide outlook, in its insight into God's heart, the only things in the Old Testament to be put in the same class with this book are the concluding chapters of the Book of Isaiah and the eighty-seventh Psalm. For in this book God appears not simply as the God of the Jews but as the God of the whole world. Here his universal love is suggested. Here we can see religion bursting through the swaddling clothes of Jewish narrowness and exclusion and claiming the world for its province. Here we get the truth asserted that the Gentiles were susceptible to and would accept the word of God. It took the vision of the great sheet and of his subsequent experience of the actual descent of the Spirit upon Cornelius and his household to convince Peter that God had granted to the Gentiles also repentance unto life. That great conviction had, however, been born in the heart of the writer of the Book of Jonah at least three centuries before: to him had been given the vision of a whole world sharing in the love and compassion of God and responsive to his call. It would do us all good to read the book over again from this point of view. If the whale incident troubles you then leave that out altogether and read directly from the fifteenth verse of the first chapter to the opening verse of chapter three, so that the central purpose of the book may be clear.

There are three great truths taught in this book that I want to call to your attention: First, God's love and compassion reach out to all people; second, all people are capable of receiving that love and responding to it; and third, people who themselves enjoy the knowledge of God are often strangely and amazingly unwilling to share it with others.

God's Universal Love

The first truth emphasized in this book is that God's love and compassion reach out to all people. That is the great revelation of the book. The Jew had been brought up to believe that he was heaven's favorite and that his people were God's peculiar people. The people outside the limits of Judaism, the people of Egypt, Assyria and Babylon, people who had often oppressed the people of Israel, were not only the enemies of the Jews; they were also the enemies of God and their end was destruction and perdition. The discovery that the prophet made under the guidance of God's Spirit was that these heathen nations were the objects of God's love and that the knowledge of God had been committed to Israel, not as a selfish possession, but that Israel might proclaim this truth to an ignorant and perishing world.

All this is implied in the opening sentence of this prophecy: "Arise, go to Nineveh, that great city, and cry against it; for their wickedness is come up before me." Nineveh was the center of that brutal kingdom of Assyria which had broken Jewish independence and deported and outraged is people. Its wickedness was great. There was no doubt about that; it had come up before God. But God had pity and compassion on Nineveh; the Ninevites were dear to him. And he would fain save them from their impending doom. "Go to Nineveh," God said, "that great city, and cry against it." All the yearning compassions of the Lord are in that verse. I sometimes think that Nineveh is taken as the scene of the prophet's ministry just because it is an extreme illustration. Its wickedness was great. If ever a people deserved punishment, the Ninevites did. But God had pity and compassion even for them. The pity that yearns over Nineveh is a pity from which none are excluded. The love that pours itself out on Nineveh is a love that extends to the lost and the last and the very least.

That is the first fact with which we must start: God's love is a universal love; his redemption is a universal redemption. He sent his Son to die for all and his mercy and compassion run out to all. This is so easily said and yet so hard to realize. It is one of those great commonplaces of religion, which just because it is commonplace, is desperately difficult really to get into our consciousness. If something could only "stab our spirits wide awake" to a realization of this truth, the missionary problem would be solved.

Let me say it quite simply and baldly: God loves everybody. He gave his Son to die for everybody. He wants to save everybody. The people of India and China, the folk of Africa, the races of New Guinea and the islands—they are all God's children; they are all in his heart and his compassion runs out to them.

This is the supreme motive for the great missionary enterprise. There are other subsidiary motives, no doubt. We are not to have missions and missionary work for the sole purpose of trade. Trade does follow the flag. But that is a poor, base, and ignoble plea. A great spiritual enterprise in the long run will fail if it is carried on for materialistic reasons.

The necessity of missionary work has been urged on humanitarian grounds. It is a noble appeal. And there is ample ground for this appeal. The dark places of the earth are full of cruelty, and the coming of Christianity emancipates people from the bondage of superstition and fear, from ignorance and disease and death. Life, for instance has become another thing for the natives of the New Hebrides since J. G. Paton first went there and for the natives of Calabar since Mary Slessor settled in their midst. Missionary work appeals to anyone and everyone who wishes to heal the open sores of humankind.

The necessity of missionary work before the war was urged in the interest of world peace. The condition of the world then and now is a call to more intense missionary effort. We will defeat Japan on the field of battle but that will not bring an end to the Japanese. They are going to play a part in the future development of the world. It is Christ or chaos. Is there any other alternative? Chaos will be the inevitable issue unless the world gets our Christ. The world debacle is a call to a new missionary crusade.

These are all motives for missions. It is back to the supreme motive we must get if missionary work is ever to become a passion with us. The other motives are prudential and humanitarian but the real missionary motive is this: that God loves all the people of the world. God loves them. God gave his son to die for them. He will not be happy until he gets his lost children back in his heart and to his home. "Arise, go unto Nineveh, that great city, and preach unto it the preaching that I bid thee" (Jonah 3:2). There you get the Father's love for his lost children and his yearning desire to save his perishing children. India is our Nineveh; China and Japan are our Nineveh; and Africa is our Nineveh. God bids us to go to Nineveh and preach the preaching he has committed to us. He bids us go and proclaim this message: "God so loved the world that he gave his only begotten Son, that whosoever believeth on him should not perish, but have everlasting life." The Father wants his children; he will not be happy in his heaven until he gathers them in. That is the great compelling motive for mission work. "The love of Christ constrains us" (2 Corinthians 5:14), said the greatest missionary of them all—not the challenge of the world, not the miseries of people (although he was not indifferent to them)—but the love of Christ. That is the supreme motive. I can conceive of no one really loving the Father without at the same time loving his children and I can conceive of no one really loving Christ without desiring to help him to gather in those for whom he gave his life.

The Capacity For Repentance

The second great truth this book illustrates and emphasizes is this: all people are capable of receiving God's love and responding to it. "Arise, go to Nineveh, that great city, and cry against it," said God to the prophet. But Jonah did not want to go, not because he thought his message beyond the comprehension of the Ninevites, not because he thought they would reject it, but because he had an uneasy feeling that on hearing it they might repent. And Jonah, hard and bitter as he was, did not want them to repent. He would have preferred to see them be the objects of God's wrath rather than the recipients of his grace. And what he feared came to pass. When, for the second time, the imperious summons came to him, "Arise, go unto Nineveh, and preach," and he went, however unwillingly, and preached to the dim multitudes of the city, "the people of Nineveh believed God." They repented, and God forgave them their sin. Nineveh, wicked Nineveh, repented. Nineveh responded to God's call. And the great and blessed truth all this symbolizes and teaches is this: none are to be shut out of the range of the gospel message. There are no unreachables or impossibles. The word, when preached and wherever preached, meets with its response. Under every form and character of human life, beneath all needs and habits, deeper than despair and more native to humanity than sin itself, lies the power of the heart to turn. It was this, and not hope, that remained at the bottom of Pandora's box when every other gift had fled. For this is the indispensable secret of hope. It lies in every heart, waiting for some dream of divine mercy to rouse it; but, when roused, neither ignorance of God, nor pride, nor long obduracy of evil may withstand it.

The power of the heart to turn is what this book asserts. The power of every human heart to turn and respond to the appeal of the divine mercy— that is the truth it proclaims. It was a noble and splendid bit of theorizing when the author wrote this book. He was arguing from the nature of God and the nature of humanity. But it is a fact of experience for us. For people have traveled to every Nineveh beneath the sun since the days of Jesus and have preached the preaching committed to them, the preaching of the grace of God in Christ, the preaching of the redeeming passion of God revealed in the Cross, and everywhere the miracle of Nineveh has been repeated, everywhere people have believed in God, and everywhere there has been demonstrated the capacity of the heart to turn.

I do not know that Christian folk have ever been reluctant to carry the gospel into any particular land for fear the people would repent. From that harsh and narrow exclusiveness which found satisfaction in the thought that other people were shut out from the mercies of God we have been delivered. But I am not at all sure that Christian people have not been slow in sending the gospel to this land and that because they felt the people could not repent. Either they said the people were so devoted to the ancestral religions that it seemed hopeless to attempt to change them or they were so sunk in savagery and sin as to be insensible to any and every high appeal. But the experience of the century and a half of modern missions has banished that doubt. Nothing has been more moving and subduing than the response the human heart everywhere makes to the preaching of the gospel. Every Nineveh can repent. They have come from the North and the South and the East and the West and have sat down in the Kingdom of God. The people who have washed their robes and made them white in the blood of the Lamb are of every nation, tribe, tongue, and condition. Everywhere, under the preaching of the gospel, there has been revealed the power of the heart to turn.

"Arise, go to Nineveh, that great city." The call came to William Carey. Nineveh to him was India, that land with an ancient religion and a hoary civilization. To some, it seemed a hopeless enterprise, so terrific was the hold their ancient religion had upon the people and so intimately had it intertwined itself with the fabric of their lives. But Indian hearts responded to the preaching of William Carey and his successors; from the devotees of Hinduism Christ gathered his converts. In that unchanging East there has been demonstrated the heart's power to turn.

"Go to Nineveh, that great city." The cry came into the ears of Robert Morrison, and as interpreted by him, Nineveh was China. It seemed a foolish adventure, for China had a civilization older than the Christian. But Chinese hearts in turn responded to the preaching of the gospel. In China, Christ gathered his confessors and martyrs. In China there has been demonstrated the heart's power to turn.

"Go to Nineveh, that great city." The call came to Robert Moffatt, and as interpreted by him, Nineveh was Africa. It seemed a desperate undertaking, to go out and seek to evangelize Africa. But Moffatt went. He went and preached in Nineveh and the heart of the African responded. Nineveh repented; in Africa Christ gathered his church. Do you remember the story of Africaner? It was a story told by Moffatt that thrilled his audiences. Africaner was a sort of robber chief in South Africa. He was the plague and peril of the white settlers in that land. He was an untamable and brutal savage. Scoffers used to tell Moffatt to convert Africaner and then they would begin to believe in missions. Moffatt went and preached his gospel to the robber chief. His coarse and brutal heart was touched. He laid aside his savagery, and before long he was accompanying Moffatt to the Cape clothed and in his right mind. Nineveh had repented. Nineveh believed God. In that brutal savage converted into a meek follower of Jesus there was demonstrated the power of the heart to turn the vilest and most degraded and brutalized heart to turn.

And that is why we omit no class, no tribe, from our missionary enterprise. There are no impossibles and unreachables. "The people of Nineveh believed God." We undertake the enterprise because the love of Christ constrains us. But we undertake it with this faith to sustain us—that there is something in every soul that cries out for Christ and responds to him when he calls. There are no people so obdurate and sunken that this faculty is destroyed in them. Nineveh, every Nineveh, can repent and believe. In every human heart there lies the power to turn.

The Reluctant Preacher

The third truth that I find in the book is that people who know the truth are often amazingly slow to impart it and to share it. Jonah was a reluctant preacher. When the call first came to him he rose up to flee unto Tarshish. He did not want to preach in Nineveh. He did not want to give Nineveh the chance to repent. He would rather see Nineveh—the capital of that brutal state that had so ruthlessly oppressed his people—destroyed than saved. So he tried to put all the land and sea that he could between himself and the great city in which God bade him preach. The religion that Jonah believed in was an exclusive, not a universal one: he rebelled against the very thought of Israel's enemies being treated as children of God.

Is this without its parallel in the life and experience of the church today? Are we not reluctant preachers still? Is it a fact that many amongst us still turn a deaf ear to God's command, "Arise, go unto Nineveh, and preach unto it the preaching that I bid thee?" We neither go ourselves nor help to send others. Nineveh, that great city, may perish for all we do to help the saving of it.

Our modern heedlessness does not arise from unwillingness as did Jonah's, although there are those amongst us who believe that the Christian religion is a religion for the West and not for the East. Our heedlessness at bottom springs from indifference. We have no concern at all for the condition of Nineveh. We are not troubled that vast sections of our world's populations live without any knowledge of Christ. We are interested in the political situation in India; we are concerned about the maintenance of the "open door" for China. But the fact that the people of India and China are ignorant of God's grace to us and all mankind in Christ has never cost us a night's sleep or given us an hour's concern. And this indifference again springs from a lack of religious experience—a failure to realize what the Christian redemption means for us. We are not filled, as the Apostle Paul was, with a sense of adoring wonder and gratitude at the grace of God in saving us. We scarcely know what it is to say in a kind of rapture of adoring awe, "The Son of God loved me and gave himself up for me." A church that has lost its sense of wonder at God's amazing love in Christ is bound to be a cold, lethargic, and indifferent church.

And that is our deepest want today—to catch again the wonder of God's redeeming love, to realize afresh what it was God did for us when he gave his Son to die on Calvary's hill. The Christian faith is not a morality—it is a redemption; it is not a philosophy—it is a salvation. It is the one who knows what redemption and salvation mean, who knows himself to be redeemed and saved by the grace of God, who will be eager to spread the gospel. It is a deepened and enriched redemption experience that is our bitter need. That is the secret of the warmed heart and the loosened tongue. And when the church gets the warmed heart and the loosened tongue there will soon be no rebellious and wicked Nineveh left; every Nineveh will repent and believe, and Christ shall see the travail of his soul be abundantly satisfied.

The Triumphant Adequacy of Christ

I am sure that, when I come unto you, I shall come in the fullness
of the blessing of the gospel of Christ. (Romans 15:29 KJV)

"See Rome and die," says the proverb. It was the dream of Paul's life to see Rome before he died. He was determined not only to see it, but to win it for Christ. The little Christian community in Rome was holding on grimly to its precarious, hard-won position, knowing that at any moment the full force of the legions of heathenism might be turned against it. Now Paul was resolved to fling himself into the attack: if it pleased God, the forlorn hope would yet become a glorious advance. He had had enough of skirmishing with paganism at its outposts; he had fought the world, the flesh, and the devil in Syria, Macedonia, and Illyricum. Now the time had come to assault the pagan principalities and powers at their headquarters, to make the foundations of Caesar's empire tremble, and to give Christ the throne.

Strange, fantastic hope. Judged by any rational standards, it was sheer absurdity. On the one side was the metropolis of the world, the heart of the empire, magnificently proud and regal on her seven hills, ruling with a rod of iron and shaking the earth with the march of her invincible legions; and on the other side, this little Jew, with his scarred face and his frail looking body, and nothing at all to offer—no credentials, no testimonials or references from important people, no imposing organization—nothing but what he called his gospel. But then to Paul, that was everything. "I am sure," he cries, "that when I come unto you, I shall come in the fullness of the blessing of the gospel of Christ." See how he loads his language, how he piles the words up, till the sentence becomes top-heavy and begins to stagger with its weight of truth: "the fullness of the blessing of the gospel of Christ." See how he reiterates and drives home his challenge four times over and every word is another hammer blow at the powers of darkness, another triumph shout of the sons of light—"the fullness of the blessing of the gospel of Christ." Here it stands today, to tell all the world what true religion is, and what is the saving might of Christianity. Let us take each of the four terms separately; and let us begin with the last.

I Am Coming to You with Christ

Not, mark you, coming with a new philosophy of life, though Rome loved dabbling in philosophy. Not coming with a new political theory, though crowds doubtless would have flocked to such a message. Not coming with a new interpretation of religion, though the intelligent community would have been immensely intrigued with that. "I am coming to you with Christ," said Paul.

It was not even "I am coming to preach righteousness, temperance, judgment"—the theme of the flaming sermon that made Felix tremble. It was not "I am come to argue with you the cause of morality," though God knew Rome needed that desperately. It was not, "I am coming to give you Christianity," though that might have seemed the most natural thing to say. It was none of these. It was this: "I am coming to you with Christ."

If ever there was a person with one subject, that person was Paul. "I determined," he told the Corinthians quite frankly, "not to know any thing among you, save Jesus Christ" (1 Corinthians 2:2). "To me," he wrote to the Philippians, "to live is Christ" (Philippians 1:21). "Life means Christ to me"—that was his one theme, given to him straight from God himself; and if ever a time should come when that is no longer the central theme of the Christian church, then the day of the church will be finished. The one thing that can justify the church is a great passion for Christ.

There have been others who have burned with the same flame as the apostle. I think of Raymond Lull, valiant missionary to the Muslims, with his oft-repeated exclamation, "I have one passion – it is he, it is he"; of Charles Wesley, singing and helping a multitude of others to sing: "Thou, O Christ, art all I want / More than all in thee I find"; of C. H. Spurgeon, crying out the secret of his life: "I looked at him, and he looked at me, and we were one forever"; of Alexander Whyte and Marcus Dods in their long Saturday walks together: "Whatever we started off with in our conversations," said Whyte, "we soon made across country, somehow, to Jesus of Nazareth." "We preach always him"; said Martin Luther, describing the message of the Reformation, "this may seem a limited and monotonous subject, likely to be soon exhausted, but we are never at the end of it."

At this moment, at ten thousand gatherings of his people, people are still, after nineteen centuries of Jesus, thinking about him, telling of his all-sufficient grace, exploring his eternal truth—and still not anywhere near the end of it. Is that not one of the strongest proofs of his divinity? Any other subject under heaven would have been exhausted long ago; this theme remains bewilderingly rich, everlastingly fresh and fertile. The early church had a strange name for Jesus. It called him the "Alpha and the Omega" which means, to put it in the language of today, that Jesus is everything in life from A to Z. There is nothing worth heralding but Jesus. "I am coming to you with Christ," said Paul. He was the man of one subject.

Why this exclusive preoccupation? After all, Rome did not want this Christ of his; what Rome wanted was help with certain concrete, practical problems. There were, for example, problems of personal relationships—stubborn, intractable problems of race, class, and family. The world, rent with strifes and hatreds and divisions, desperately needed a truer fellowship and a more enduring peace. "I offer you Christ" said Paul. Might not the world have retorted, "But you don't understand. It is not that we want. Stop being irrelevant." There was also the problem of moral control. A multitude of hearts, torn with the lusts of the flesh, cried inarticulately for self-mastery. "I offer you Christ" said Paul. Again, might not the world have retorted, "Man, you do not understand. You are off the track. It is not what we are asking for. We want self-control." Why then with all these different and definite problems in front of him—racial, social, political, and ethical—did Paul keep harping on the one note CHRIST, CHRIST, CHRIST?

Let us see this in the light of our modern situation. Why keep to the one note today? This is where the critics of the gospel strike. "Leave that played-out message," they demand, "that refuge from hard facts, that pathetic strumming out the one old theme. We don't deny the truth or the historicity of the story of Jesus. What we do deny is its relevance to the present world-scene. Let us come to grips with actualities and do something. Why all this talk of Christ?"

Can we meet that? Assuredly we can. They tell us Jesus is simply irrelevant today. We dare to maintain that Paul's way—"I offer you Christ"—is still, after nineteen centuries, the one and only way of hope. Take our most pressing problems. Take the frightful difficulty of living together in the world, the agelong, urgent problem of personal relationships between person and person, between race and race. What is the best way to deal with that? Is it to preach brotherhood? Is it to beg and beseech men to love one another and be friends? That leads nowhere. And why? Because it is attacking the problem from the wrong end. But now, suppose that you begin at the other end. Suppose you start farther back. Suppose that some at least of the toil and energy now being put into the effort to promote brotherhood on a purely natural basis could be turned into another channel altogether. Suppose you bring people face to face with God in Christ.

Suppose that they feel the impact of Jesus and come under the spell of Jesus. Then the other thing we are after, the fellowship for which we long, begins to come of its own accord. It comes as a by-product. Thus the problem solves itself because souls that are in true and vital union with Jesus develop a tone and color in which fellowship, so far from being impossible, has become inevitable. Christ irrelevant? He is the one fully relevant fact in life today.

So it is with all the other problems that vex the heart of this troubled world, our own moral problems included. The weary business of trying, by Herculean efforts of will, to eliminate evils and cultivate virtues is always in the long run futile. It is starting at the wrong end of things. The other end is the place to begin—and the other end is the grace of Christ. Here is David Brainerd describing, in that wonderful journal of his, the method of his work among the Native Americans in our country: "I never got away from Jesus, and Him crucified; and I found that when my people were gripped by this, I had no need to give them instructions about morality. I found that one followed as the sure and inevitable fruit of the other."

Yes indeed; for Jesus, once known and understood and loved, brings with him into a person's life a different atmosphere in which spontaneously the evil things begin to droop and the fine things burst into bloom. Christ irrelevant? He is as relevant to every one of us, in our deepest and most intimate need, as the daily bread we have to eat to keep ourselves alive.

Christianity, therefore, is right, absolutely right, when it refuses, in spite of a barrage of criticism, to be deflected from the one object for which it exists, which is to hold up Jesus. It must be the most hopeless, sterile, soul-destroying thing imaginable to have only arguments, advice, and moral points of view to offer to the world to help in its troubles. But to have Christ to offer—a living and accessible an all-sufficient Christ—how different that is, how redemptively effective, how gloriously charged with hope. "I am coming to you with Christ" said Paul.

I Am Coming to You with the Gospel of Christ

"Gospel" means "tidings, news, good news." Not views, mind you, but news. The substitute of views for news is one of the most damaging and deadening things that can happen to religion. Sometimes the church itself has become infected with error, and has been so preoccupied with human views of God that there has been little time or energy left for heralding God's news to humans. What is the news? "There is only one piece of news that I know," said a good woman to Tennyson, when the poet on a journey had arrived at her house and inquired if anything of note were happening, "Christ died for all men." "Well" said Tennyson, "that is old news, and good news, and new news." Is that not your one feeling every time you open your New Testament? Like the great runner Pheidippides bringing to Athens the news of the victory of Marathon, those men and women of Jesus were carrying a message from the battle fought out to a finish at Calvary; and wherever they passed, through city street or country road, one cry they had for all they met—"Tidings, good tidings. The greatest of all good tidings—God and sinners reconcile." Hearts by the thousands were thrilled to hear it. It was glorious news, the like of which they had never listened to before.

But today, "Christ died for us;" says H. G. Wells, "do we care?" "I suppose that Christ died for the world," says someone apathetically, "but then it is such an old and time-worn story. You really cannot blame us if we take it pretty calmly."

There have been days, thank God, when the news of Christ meant so much to people that they could not keep their voices steady when they spoke his blessed name. But we take calmly even his crown of thorns and his pierced hands and his sweat of blood. Yet in the deepest sense, this fact of Jesus crucified, dead and buried, risen and exalted, is news still, tidings that are nothing less than startling. And if we are not startled it can only be because the meaning of the fact has not been apprehended.

Think of what is involved. Take a saying like this: "I can do all things through Christ which strengtheneth me." Take the fact of a person, once broken and defeated and helpless, yet now standing on his feet, with head up, with level eyes confronting life, danger, furious opposition, and death crying, "I can do all things through Christ." Now that in essence is Christianity. And do you not see that if that is what Christ is aiming at, and if in spite of it we are content to plod along our undistinguished road, with things perhaps holding us down in captivity today that were holding us down ten years ago, then Christ's offer is news indeed, astonishing and startling news?

Or take the great cry of Easter morning, "Christ is risen. Christ is not here." That again is Christianity. And do you not think that if that is true then a good many of us have yet to experience something of what Dr. Dale of Birmingham experienced one day in his study when he was writing an Easter sermon for his people? Halfway through his work, the thought of the Risen Lord broke in upon him as it had never done before. "Christ is alive," he said to himself, "alive!" Then he paused. "Alive!" he cried again.

"Living as really as I myself am." And he got up and walked about, repeating "Christ is living, Christ is living." It had come upon him with a burst of sudden glory—Christ risen and alive and at his side. And for multitudes of professing Christians that is news still, startling news.

Or turn to the Sermon on the Mount, calling to us down the centuries to love our enemies, to go on loving even when spoken against and hurt and misrepresented, to love as Christ did, right through to the end. That is Christianity—the belief that this, impossible as it seems, can veritably by the grace of God be put into practice. And if that is true—not as is so often hinted the poetic license of an overheated piety, not something to be explained away by ingenious commentators or neutralized by a mass of exceptions, but really true, something which Jesus intended men to take just as He spoke it and to act upon, working it into the very fiber and constitution of the world—then, I say again, over great areas of life today his gospel is news, startling news.

Or take what is really the core of the Christian Gospel, the doctrine of the forgiveness of sins. That is the distinctive glory of Christianity. But for so many of us it is still just a doctrine, an article in a creed, a bit of rather ponderous theological lumber. Yet here are those people of the New Testament singing and reveling about it. Why? Was that just silly emotionalism? That is the last charge that can fairly be brought against the members of the early church: their logic was levelheaded and irrefragable. Why then, were they so excited? Because forgiveness means this amazing thing—the complete and perfect healing of a relationship that seemed irretrievably spoiled and damaged. It means that the uneasy, guilty feelings which trouble the mind and haunt the memory can be utterly transmuted. It means, for all who are penitent, an unconditional new beginning. It could mean your going away from this church this morning with every barrier between God and your own soul completely broken down. It could mean life's most precious relationship put gloriously and decisively right. It could mean, where that relationship is concerned, your facing life now without one care in the world. And do you not see that, if that is true—and as sure as Christ died, it is true—then for multitudes today it is news, exhilarating, magnificent news?

And yet they tell us this Christianity is an old story, tried out for nineteen centuries and exhausted. If the gospel consisted of people's views and notions, that verdict might be right. But the gospel is not humanity's theorizing about God: it is God's news to humanity. There is no exhausting that. "I am coming to you," said Paul, "with the gospel—the good news of Christ."

I Am Coming to You with the Blessing
of the Gospel of Christ

Here the suggestion is the reaction of religion upon life, its practical effect on the concerns of every common day. It makes life blessed, says the apostle; it lights up a person's entire experience with joy, peace, courage, and serenity.

With one voice all the saints proclaim that there is no nook or cranny of life that is not crowned with light and flooded with sunshine, no dull stretch of the road that does not grow romantic, no common task or lonely way that is not marvelously transfigured, no human friendship that is not hallowed, no heavy cross which does not begin to shine with glory, when once Christ and his glad tidings have gripped and held the heart.

All the saints have proved it. Paul and Silas proved it, lying with torn backs and bleeding heads in the Philippian dungeon, for even that grim shambles of a place could not smother the joy that broke into songs at the midnight hour. Francis of Assisi proved it. Who that has read the story of the Christian centuries does not love St. Francis? And why? Because it is the man's gallant joyfulness that grips you, the joy which sang its way in beggar's clothes round Italy, earning for him that blithesome and most honorable name, "God's Troubadour." The joy grips you that leapt like fire from his soul to a thousand others, till tens of thousands had been kindled at its torch, and a dead church, feeling that the winter was past them and the time for the singing of the birds had come, broke from its sleep in sudden resurrection; the joy that at the last went down into the valley of the shadow of death singing and passed singing to the throne of God. . . . And the secret of it? The blessing of the gospel of Christ.

General Booth and the Salvation Army have proved it. The driving power of that great movement that has seen so many miracles of grace is its indwelling joy, the radiant overflowing happiness of ordinary folk who, having themselves been caught by love's strong arms out of the toils of sin, really know, as a vivid and most personal experience, the amazing difference Christ can make. Nor is there one of us who may not prove for himself that true blessedness, by which I mean real solid happiness, quietness, poise, and dignity, freedom from nerves, restlessness and the worried, hectic attitude that is so common today. The power of a spirit genuinely liberated and at peace is in our grasp, since Christ is here and the most burdened heart amongst us now can go forth from the place of prayer reinforced, resolute, and calm and clothed with the gladness of God. "I am coming," said Paul, "with the blessing of the gospel of Christ."

I Am Coming to You with the Fullness of the Blessing of the Gospel of Christ

For some of us that is the crux of things. We have the blessing of the gospel of Christ and we thank God for that. Nothing is going to be allowed to rob us of that and yet, is there not a dim feeling that we have never quite entered into the fullness of the blessing? Something has come to us from our religion; much that we treasure dearly has come to us out of the bosom of our Christian faith. Yet there is something lacking, some final gift of God unappropriated, some last step untaken, some deepest secret unprobed. There is many a person today who prays to God in the name of Jesus and would feel utterly lost if robbed of prayer, yet there is something missing. He joins in worship, loves the old hymns, finds that they help and speak to his need, yet there is something lacking. He is aware that Jesus can give absolute victory in the moral sphere, yet he has never been absolutely victorious. He knows that Jesus can keep the human heart in the very peace of God, yet he still gets worried. He is sure that Jesus can raise a man above the clamor of tongues and the opinions of the world, yet he has never been raised above them. He has the blessing, but not the fullness of the blessing. So he lacks that feeling of release and spontaneity, that steadfastness and buoyancy and dignity, that God intended that he have.

To that one we say, "One thing thou lackest: you have not committed your all to God. Whatever it may be, put it all on the altar of God. Do it now. Now is the time of confession and consecration."

Is this the word of God today to some of us? One sin retained, and all the rest of life's glory dimmed in consequence; one corner barricaded against Christ, and all the rest reduced in Christian efficiency; one secret hugged from God, and a shadow over all the sunshine; one heavenly vision disobeyed, and the soul's gloaming gathering in; one weak moral compromise accepted, and all the lights of religion lowered and the full blessing never known—is that what Christ sees, looking now to you and me? Then the next step lies with us. Down with the barrier! Away with reservations! Be done with the misery of a divided soul! Offer the whole sacrifice upon the altar of God! So shall we have no longer an impoverished religion and a deficient moral dynamic but the living and limitless blessing in the God-created splendor of its fullness.

After Easter

This is now the third time that Jesus was manifested to the disciples, after that he was risen from the dead. (John 21:14 ASV)

I am not going to speak about this appearance of our Lord to the disciples on the Sea of Tiberias from the account from which the verse of my text is taken. Exquisite though the story is I am not going to say a word about it in this sermon. Nor am I going to take up any time in discussing the text. Commentators have discussed and debated that phrase "the third time" to no end. They have wondered what the Evangelist's method of reckoning was, for already in the previous chapter he has recorded three appearances of the risen lord. I will content myself with stating what my own belief is. The Evangelist here is ignoring the appearances of the risen Lord to individuals, such as his appearances to Mary and to Peter and to the two disciples on the way to Emmaus. The appearances he has in mind are the appearances of Christ to the whole body of disciples or to considerable groups of them. Of these his appearance in the upper room on Easter evening was the first; his further appearance in the same place to the same group with Thomas added was the second. So this appearance to this group of seven at the Sea of Tiberias was the third. That is the only word by way of exegesis that I am going to make.

My real text is that last phrase: "after that he was risen from the dead." The ecclesiastical description of this Sunday is "the first Sunday after Easter." We are quite aware that last Sunday was Easter Sunday, and that this is the first Sunday after Easter. But that little phrase "after Easter" laid hold of my mind. What does that mean? It is not simply this Sunday but every Sunday and everything in it that is "after Easter." Easter is more than a date on the calendar; Easter is an event that has changed the color of human life and altered the current of the world's history. We live in an "after Easter" world.

There are certain great and catastrophic events which seem radically to alter the whole scheme of things and to start the world on a new career. The Great War [World War I] was such an event. We know that things have changed greatly since the last war and we can expect even greater changes from this conflagration and deluge of blood. We have seen and realized that changes have taken place morally. The old ideas and ideals and conventions no longer apply. The message of the poets no longer possesses its lofty idealism. The message of the pulpit has undergone a great change. Where once we were concerned with doctrine and numbers, now we are working at the task of practical Christian living. The world has changed economically. Our fiscal system is being altered. Individualism seems to be on its deathbed and a steady process of socializing is going on. I am not concerned today with whether these changes are good or bad. But I do say that they have given a new set to the world's life. This world in a real sense is a new world.

But the changes that we spoke of are nothing compared to the change effected by the resurrection of Jesus. The difference between the old order and the new order is to be compared with the difference of the world before Easter and after Easter. No event in the world's history has had such profound and far-reaching effects as the resurrection of Jesus. The world "before Easter" as compared with the world "after Easter" is a new world. I want to illustrate, and by illustrating to justify, that statement.

The Sunday

Literally speaking, today is not the first Sunday after Easter. There have been thousands and thousands of "after Easter" Sundays. All the Sundays have been "after Easter" Sundays. There wasn't a Sunday before Easter. There has been a Sunday ever since. For Sunday, let us remember, is not the old Jewish Sabbath. The old Jewish Sabbath, with the rest of the Mosaic Law, was fulfilled in Christ. Sunday is a new institution, a happier, gladder, and more joyous day that the old Jewish Sabbath. This is the day on which our Lord rose from the dead. This is the day on which he appeared to his disciples to turn their sorrow into joy. This is the day on which he came again for the sake of Thomas and showed him his hands and his side and turned his doubt into adoring faith. This is the day on which he came back in the Spirit to his disciples as they were gathered together in the Upper Room never again to leave them. This is the Lord's Day.

I do not know that our Lord left any instructions about observing Sunday. But instinctively, somehow, the Christian church came to observe this day as its day of rest and worship. It may be that the Jewish Christians, in the early days at any rate, observed the Jewish Sabbath as well. But in the Gentile churches from the very start, and gradually throughout the whole of the Christian church, Sunday became the day when the Christians assembled themselves together. It was on the first day of the week that the little Christian community in Troas met together to break bread. It was on the first day of the week that Paul exhorted the Christians of Corinth to make their gifts to the poor. It was on the Lord's Day, while he was a prisoner on Patmos, that the Apostle John was in the Spirit and heard and saw such wonderful things. "Each Lord's Day," says the *Teaching of the Twelve*, "exhort Christian folk to come together and break bread and give thanks."[1] Every Sunday is an "after Easter" Sunday. There was never a Sunday before; there has been a Sunday ever since. I am not at all surprised that Dr. [Robert William] Dale used to begin every Sunday morning service with an Easter hymn. Every Sunday is a commemoration of Easter and every Sunday is a product of the mighty Easter event.

People take Sunday very much as a matter of course, almost as an event in the course of nature. As a matter of simple fact, it is a creation and monument of Christian faith. Every Sunday is "after Easter" and this unbroken line of Sundays makes a long chain of witnesses to the reality of our Lord's Resurrection. They date back in unbroken sequence to his empty grave. They are all "after Easter."

The Gospels

The Gospels are also "after Easter." Scholars have devoted an immense amount of labor to the task of trying to fix the dates of the Gospels. They have tried to settle the question of order: which of the Synoptic Gospels was written first and might therefore be regarded as providing the basis for the others? Some believe that the ultimate sources of the Synoptic Gospels were a primitive Mark and a document containing certain sayings of Jesus. Today our modern critical scholars have gone farther than that by saying that they can separate out the various documents that have gone into the makeup of our Gospels. I have no criticism to pass upon their work except that sometimes they make me feel that they are not seeing the forest for the trees. Scholarship is not to be feared but is rather to be welcomed. Criticism can do nothing against the truth but only for it. As a matter of fact, the latest criticism is inclined to give the Fourth Gospel an earlier date and far more historic value than the scholarship of twenty-five years ago.

But though scholars give various dates to the various Books of the New Testament, there is one date that fits them all: they are all dated "after Easter." That is their real date. Scholarship must be allowed to decide whether they were written in the fifties or the sixties or the seventies of the first century. That is a matter of small moment. Their real date is "after

---

[1][*Didache* 14.1.]

Easter." What I mean is this: there would not have been a Gospel, there would not have been a Book of Acts, there would not have been a single letter of Peter or John or Paul, but for the Resurrection. You must remember that Christianity was in existence before a line of the New Testament was written. It was not the Gospels and Epistles that created faith in the resurrection; it was the Resurrection of Jesus that called into being the Gospels and the Epistles. The men who wrote the books of the New Testament lived and moved and had their being in the glorious sunshine of the Resurrection. That is what the latest school of scholarship is saying: that what we have in the New Testament is the reflection of the faith of the early church.

One thing is certain: if there had been no resurrection there would have been no New Testament. If the story of Jesus had ended at the Cross and the grave there never would have been a New Testament. If the story stopped with those words "crucified, dead, and buried" there never would have been a New Testament. As one writer put it,

> It is not this or that in the New Testament—it is not the story of the empty tomb, or of the appearing of Jesus in Jerusalem or Galilee— which is the primary evidence for the Resurrection; it is the New Testament itself. The life that throbs in it from beginning to end, the life that always fills us again with wonder as it beats upon us from its pages, is the life which the Risen Saviour has quickened in Christian souls.[2]

The New Testament is dated "after Easter." Consider the place the New Testament occupies in the thoughts of people. Think of the influence it has had in shaping people's ideals and in educating their consciences. Is it not the New Testament which has been dictating the progress of the centuries? Isn't that the history of our Western civilization, a constant if fumbling effort to put its precepts into practice in the individual, industrial, national, and international life?

Was I wrong in saying that the Resurrection was the most tremendous event in the history of the world? It gave us the New Testament! The New Testament is an "after Easter" book.

----

[2][James Denney, "The Historical Basis of the Christian Faith: The Resurrection of Jesus," in *Jesus and the Gospel: Christianity Justified in the Mind of Christ* (New York: Eaton & Mains; Cincinnati: Jennings & Graham, 1908) 101.]

The Church

Or think of the Christian church. When did the Christian church have its beginning? The answer is, "after Easter." There was no church before Easter. There has been a church ever since. There never would have been a church but for Easter. Had the Cross been the end of Jesus, I wonder sometimes whether we should ever have heard of his name. It is just possible, of course, that some of his disciples might have written down some of his wonderful sayings and told us something about his career, just as Xenophon and Plato have written down their recollections about Socrates and his sayings. I am not at all sure about that, though. These disciples had cherished expectations about Jesus that no one cherished about Socrates. When Socrates drank the hemlock his friends were grieved, but they didn't feel they had been disappointed and cheated in him. But that is exactly how the disciples of Jesus would have felt if the Cross had been his end. That is indeed how they did feel during those two days when he lay dead and buried in Joseph's rocky grave. They felt they had been deceived, misled, and cheated. They had followed Jesus in the belief that he was God's Messiah but he had ended not on a throne but on a cross. The disciples felt that they had made a mistake when they left all and followed him. They had blundered. They had wasted three years. They had exposed themselves to the ridicule of their fellows. Men in that frame of mind would scarcely be likely to perpetuate the memory of one who had so tragically disappointed them. To perpetuate his memory would be to perpetuate the remembrance of their own mistake and folly. No. If Jesus had finished his life at the cross, I think the disciples would have wished to forget him and the whole episode of their mistaken discipleship as soon as possible. If Jesus had finished his career upon the cross, I question very much whether we should ever have heard of his name.

This is true at any rate: had Jesus finished upon the cross, there never would have been a Christian church. The disciples on that Friday and Saturday were in a mood of utter despair. A common disappointment held them together during these days, but if nothing had happened when the Passover was over, they would have stolen back to their homes in Galilee and gone back to their old occupations and that would have been the end of the Jesus movement. But on the third day something tremendous happened. Their Master, whom they had seen crucified, was seen alive by them. With that tremendous happening the church was born. The church's date, like the New Testament's date, is "after Easter."

The writer of a book entitled *The Shining Mystery of Jesus*[3] declared that if all the gospels were broken off where apparently Mark broke off, at the discovery of the empty tomb, and if St. Paul's account of the various appearances had never been written, and if the opening verses of the Book of Acts had been lost, we should then have been left without any account of the Resurrection. But even in such a case, he said, we would be driven to postulate some tremendous event to account for the difference between the followers of Jesus who fled in panic and despair on Good Friday and those same followers who a short time later astonished the Jewish leaders by their boldness and courage that did not flinch even in face of persecution and death. Something great must have happened to transfigure timidity into heroism. They themselves say that tremendous fact was the resurrection of the crucified Christ.

It was that fact that made the church; there never would have been a church without it, for the church is made by its Gospel and exists to preach its Gospel. But what Gospel would it possess apart from the Resurrection? I am not surprised that, so long as they thought that Jesus was dead, the disciples kept themselves locked up in that upper room for fear of the Jews. There was no temptation to go out and preach. What was there to preach about? They could only have spoken of their disappointment and their shattered hopes. But "after Easter" no bolts or bars could keep those men in the upper room. No threats of the Sanhedrin could frighten them into silence. They had a mighty Gospel to proclaim. They had good tidings to announce. They had to tell the people that, in Jesus, God's Messiah had appeared for the redemption and salvation of his people. It was the resurrection that made them sure of that. The resurrection gave them their Gospel and their Gospel made them into a church. The church is an "after Easter" creation. It was made by the Resurrection and it lives by its present-day experience of the living Christ. So it is no exaggeration to say that the chief evidence for the resurrection of Jesus Christ is the fact of the Christian church.

Consider again the place the church has occupied in the world's life and the work the church has done and is still doing. I am not suggesting for one moment that the church is free from fault. Even if I were tempted to think so, there are so many critics who are all eager to tell me how great and

---

[3][Douglas Allen Edwards, *The Shining Mystery of Jesus* (New York: Longmans, Green, 1928).]

grievous are the church's shortcomings that I should not be allowed to cherish the delusion long. I know the church has her defects and shortcomings. I know that she has often blundered. I know that she has often failed to do what she ought to do. Yet, for all that, I will maintain that the Christian church has been and is the most beneficent society in the world. I will maintain that the moral betterment of the world is due to the Christian church. I will maintain that to this day the church is the mainspring of all ameliorative moments. Was I wrong, then, in saying that the Resurrection was the most tremendous event in the world's history, seeing that it created the Christian church? The date of the Christian church, like the date of the New Testament, is "after Easter."

The New Outlook

For my last illustration of the change that Easter has made, let me speak for a moment of the new outlook on death and the beyond. The great difference between the world before Easter and the world after Easter is that the eventide of the one world was shadowed and dark while the eventide of the other is radiant with light. If we could have compared the inscriptions in some pre-Christian cemetery with the new kind of inscriptions written on the graves in the catacombs the difference would at once flash upon us. Sadness characterizes the one and immortal hope the other. What accounts for the difference? Just this: the catacomb inscriptions are "after Easter." Do you remember how Bunyan describes the coming of the Post to Mr. Ready to Halt? It has an exquisite touch in it. This is what the Post said to that lame and crippled Pilgrim: "My message is to tell thee that thy Lord expects thee at His table to sup with Him in His Kingdom the next day after Easter." It is only the day "after Easter" that warrants someone in cherishing such a hope as that. Before Easter people went out into the dark, without a hope to cheer the tomb. But "after Easter" they looked forward to sit at the King's table and sup with him in his kingdom. I do not forget that "before Easter" some people faced the end with courage and unblanched face. But it is only "after Easter" they have been able to triumph in and over death. "To depart and be with Christ is far better" is an "after Easter" word. "O grave, where is thy victory? O death, where is thy sting?" is an "after Easter" shout.

A religious newspaper some time ago printed a series of Easter messages. Let me quote one of them. It is an incident related by one who was a chaplain in the Great War. "When I was in France in 1916, I was called to a case just put on the danger list. I found a young man mortally wounded. I opened my Bible and began to read a passage, but he stopped me and said, 'Not that. Please read where it says, "The trumpet shall sound and the dead shall be raised incorruptible and we shall be changed." ' I was thrilled, says the chaplain, by the note of triumph in his voice." The Post came to him as to Mr. Ready to Halt, the day "after Easter."

"After Easter." Yes, it is true, Easter transfigured the world. I do not know whether we always realize the difference Easter has made. I do not know that we always live as if the world has had an Easter. But let us this day rejoice that we live in the "after Easter" world, a world blessed with Sunday, the New Testament, and the Christian church. Let us rejoice that we live in a world in which death has lost its terror because we know that it is not the end but a new beginning when mortality is swallowed up by life.

Part 6

The Family

The Measure of a Home

And thou shall write them upon the posts of thy house.
(Deuteronomy 6:9 KJV)

A London magazine once asked their subscribers to define a home. More than one thousand replies were received and out of that number six were selected as the best definitions of a home.

Home – a world of strife shut out, a world of love shut in.

Home – a place where the small are great and the great are small.

Home – the father's kingdom, the mother's world, and the child's paradise.

Home – the place where we grumble the most and are treated the best.

Home – the center of our affection, through which our heart's best wishes twine.

Home – the place where our stomachs get three square meals a day and our hearts a thousand.

The home is all this but it is a great deal more. It is important that the home be magnified through the media of the press and the radio. It is far more important that the church magnify the home with all of its Christian significance and meaning. Our homes are under constant pressure and are seriously threatened by the events of our day and thus they need the moral and spiritual understanding and undergirding of the Christian Gospel. What are some of the elements that make up a Christian home?

A Place of Re-creation

The Christian home is a haven of restoration for the members of the family. One day two men were talking and one of them said that his shoes were too tight and that his feet were hurting. The other man asked him why he did not take his shoes off. He replied: "Listen, when I get home tonight supper won't be ready and if it is it won't be fit to eat. It isn't bad enough I've gotta look at my mother-in-law but I've got to listen to her too. My daughter married a man I cannot stand, and they have got four of the meanest kids I ever saw. My loafin' brother-in-law will be sitting in the only easy chair in the house, and the only pleasure I have when I get home is taking off these tight shoes."

We may well pity that poor chap for his house is not a home. We pity all those whose homes are more like an armed camp of unhappy experiences, petty bickering, and crosspatch criticism. Too often our homes become places of endless controversies and arguments, dull monotony and careless differences to the niceties of life.

Our homes deserve better treatment than that. We owe them our best, not our worst. We owe them not merely our best furniture but our best manners, best interests, best conversation, and best friendships. Too often we display our worst tempers and attitudes in the home. God knows that our souls are often beaten and exhausted with the experiences of life. We need relaxation and recuperation. Homes are to provide these. Homes that specialize in this function are glorious and blessed.

One lady tells about a new maid who from morning till night listened to endless soap operas on the kitchen radio to the distraction of her mistress. When the maid was told to turn the radio off, she immediately gave notice that she was quitting, explaining with dignity, "I do not care to work in a home where there are no cultural influences." Options as to cultural influences may differ. In furnishing our homes with modern gadgetry we must not forget the most important cultural influences. These include old-fashioned love and understanding, laughter and loyalty, comradeship and kindness, honesty and patience, prayer and faith. These are the things that restore the tattered spirits of men and women, weary and injured in the work and worry of life. Modern men and women sorely need the healing of spirit and comfort of soul that can be found only in the sacred precincts of a home enriched with sympathy, understanding, and forgiveness. In such homes men and women and children discover the secret of great and serene living. No price is too great to make them so.

An Outpost of National Security

The Christian home is an outpost of national security. Justice Birdseye for the New York Supreme Court said in 1857, "The family is the origin of all society and of all government. The whole frame of governments and laws has been said to exist only to protect and support the family." The totalitarian state, however, challenges the importance of the family to society. It seeks to break down the family unit as neither biologically necessary nor politically desirable. Unfortunately we in America are carelessly aiding the Communist program by an evident undermining of family life. Divorce breaks up almost one out of every three marriages. Sex delinquency and juvenile delinquency break up family relationships. The state is assuming more and more of the functions of family support, health, and old age security. No wonder some sociologists are predicting the end of the family system.

This must not be so, for with the degeneration of the family will go the destruction of the democratic state. The wealth and power of this nation do not consist in its farms, forests, factories, and fortunes, but in the character of the homes of the people. In all our concern about defenses against the atomic and hydrogen bombs we need to know that the Christian home is the first line of defense. Nowhere can we make a greater contribution to the preservation of human freedom and the defense of human rights than right in our homes. In the atmosphere of Christian idealism they can be places where moral character is developed, where the rights of others are recognized, and where the authority of love is respected. Homes of free people should encourage the disciplines of cooperative living and foster the qualities of self-reliance and independence. Homes like this are the hope of the nation.

Grace Noll Crowell said:

So long as there are homes to which men turn
At the close of day;
So long as there are homes where children are—
Where women stay,
If love and loyalty and faith be found
Across those sills,
A stricken nation can recover from
Its gravest ills.

So long as there are homes where fires burn
And there is bread,
So long as there are homes where lamps are lit
And prayers are said;
Although a people falters through the dark
And nations grope,
With God himself back of these little homes
We still can hope.[1]

---

[1][Grace Noll Crowell, "So Long as There Are Homes" (n.d.) as now in *Poems of Inspiration and Courage. The Best Verse of Grace Noll Crowell* (New York: Harper & Row, 1965) 195.]

A Background for Personal Achievement

The Christian home is a background for personal achievement and service. Roger Babson said:

> I have not been able to find a single useful institution which has not been founded by either an intensely religious man or by the son of a praying father or a praying mother. I have made this statement before the chambers of commerce of all the largest cities of the country and have asked them to bring forward a case that is an exception to this rule. Thus far, I have not heard of a single one.

More that that, it may be said that the large majority of outstanding men and women who have made significant contributions to society have come out of great Christian home backgrounds.

It is in plain homes, simple homes, God-fearing homes, homes of faith and prayer, that dreams are kindled and the qualities of courage, sacrifice, and industry are developed that make people great in character, achievement, and service. Thank God for homes like that today. God save us from homes of selfish snobbishness and help us to make of our homes rich and wholesome backgrounds for lives of useful leadership. For Christian homes dare not be homes of self-interest but rather must be homes that make a creative contribution to Christian society.

A Laboratory of Christian Living

The Christian home is a laboratory of Christian living. If there is one supreme function of the Christian home, it is the building of Christian idealism and moral character into the lives of the children and young people. Because of the secularism of our public schools and the scattered opportunities of our Bible schools, the home must have a large part in fostering the spirit of Christ in the lives of youth or it will not be done. Too many of our young people are growing up to be modern pagans because mothers are too busy with their clubs and fathers are too busy making a living to be bothered with the religious training of their children. We cannot expect our children to have moral stamina or ethical principles, to say nothing of vision or understanding of the Christian faith or life, when parents are completely indifferent to Christian ideals for the home. Unless Christian influences can offset the damaging effects of liquor, trashy comic books, cheap radio and television programs, of loose shows and movies, the results are all to apparent. The F.B.I. reports that boys and girls under voting age account for thirty-five per cent of the thieves, fifteen per cent of the murderers, and sixty-one per cent of the car thieves of the nation. Two million of our young men and women are infected annually with social diseases. Of the one million babies born out of wedlock in recent years 60,000 of them were born to girls under fourteen years of age. All this is to say nothing of the unhappiness and personality defects of those whose training ignores God.

There have been improvements in working, living, health, and educational conditions in the past thirty years. The fact remains, however, that such environmental factors as bathrooms, convertibles, air conditioning, and vitamin pills cannot themselves produce better men and women. There must be a like improvement in moral character and spiritual experience. This is the job of the Christian home. It is not the kind of house but the kind of home that matters.

There is one way and only one way to make the spirit of Jesus Christ a functioning and guiding ideal at the center of the home life. We don't need the preacher to tell us that. Every mother of the year selected by the Golden Rule Foundation has said the same thing. Divorce court judges and social workers say it. When Mrs. Clara T. Murray was honored for twenty-five years in probation work in Chicago, she gave three simple rules for young people to stay out of trouble. (1) Make your mother your friend and companion. (2) Keep out of taverns and nightclubs. (3) Never forget your religious training. These rules were drawn from working with 108,750 cases.

Editorial writers are saying it. Business institutions are saying it. For several years the Institute of Life Insurance has run a full-page ad in 375 newspapers pointing up the need for religion in the home. It shows a picture of a mother hearing the bedtime prayers of her two children. The ad carries the words: "We teach our children our faith so that they will not be alone as they face the world." The sponsors say they have never before had such a tremendous response to any publicity.

We must renew a spirit of deep spiritual dedication to God in our homes if they are to perform their high functions. A bishop was once making an appeal for funds before a native congregation in India. A poor widow wrote on her card, "I will give Christ six annas and my baby boy." The money amounted to twelve cents, and the infant was only one in India's millions. Yet the widow never forgot that her child was dedicated. She raised him in a vital Christian faith in an unchristian land. Now a man, that child is one of the great Christian leaders of India. There was the American father of little means but great faith whose simple will contained this statement:

> I desire to bequeath to my children and their families my testimony to the truth and preciousness of the Gospel of Jesus Christ. This heritage of the Christian faith is of infinitely more value than any house, land, or barns. I hereby bequeath and devise it to them.

And then there is the prayer of the mother after the children had gone to bed:

> They are asleep, O God, and I am tired. Make me all I want them to be, strong, and true, and greathearted. Let me mend their souls as will as attend their bodies. Help me to learn the secret of trust in thee from their trust in me.

From such great dedications come great homes.

The Portrait of a Godly Mother

Scripture: Proverbs 31:10-31; Revelation 21:1-7
Text: *A woman that feareth the Lord, she shall be praised.*
(Proverbs 31:30 KJV)

The closing verses of the book of Proverbs contain a full-length portrait of a godly mother. The Book of Proverbs is the only book in the Bible especially written for young folk. In fact, the book is addressed mainly to one young man. It affords a practical theory of a planned life with commonsense ways of living in a workaday world. At the end of the book a beautiful poem sings the praises of a godly mother. Such an upright woman,

A creature not too bright or good
For human nature's daily food,[1]

affords an object lesson of all the ideals and the duties set forth in the Book of Proverbs.

The poem takes the form of an acrostic. The Hebrew alphabet contains twenty-two letters. Hence the poem consists of that many parts, which we know as verses. Originally the aim must have been to encourage the growing boy in committing the words to memory. Even afterward he would have in his heart an ideal of the one whom he ought some day to wed—

Whoe'er she be—
That not impossible She,
That shall command my heart and me.[2]

In some other home, perhaps nearby, a growing lass would learn by heart the same golden verses from the Proverbs. Then she would have ever in view a worthy ideal of what she ought to become: "A woman that feareth

---

[1][William Wordsworth, "Perfect Woman" (or "She was a phantom of delight," 1804), *The Oxford Book of English Verse 1250–1918*, new edition, ed. Arthur Quiller-Couch (New York, Toronto: Oxford University Press, 1939; [1]1900) #543, lines 17-18.]

[2][Richard Crashaw, "Wishes to His Supposed Mistress" (1646?), *The Oxford Book of English Verse 1250–1918*, new edition, ed. Arthur Quiller-Couch (New York, Toronto: Oxford University Press, 1939; [1]1900) #345, lines 1-3.]

the Lord, she shall be praised." Here, then, we have a full-length portrait of a godly woman.

The Charm of a Godly Woman

In this biblical "word painting" the subject of the study by the master artist is a woman of the Martha type. According to the Scriptures, the Lord Jesus loved both Martha and Mary. Both in religion and in life there should be room and a welcome for the sisters of Mary, gentle and mild, lovers of beauty and loyal to God. But at present we are to think about the larger throng, the daughters of Martha.

The heroine of our poem appears as a good woman of the Hebrew type. That sort of everyday saint has often arisen among the Scottish and the Dutch. The reason may be that such sturdy folk have reared their little ones on simple fare, often including porridge and proverbs. The woman before us works with zeal, and her strength never falters. She undertakes routine tasks with wisdom and care. In fact, she serves as an object lesson of those vanishing virtues once known as Puritan: foresight, industry, and thrift.

Better still, this patron saint of old-time Hebrew women excels in the fine art of friendship. "She stretcheth out her hand to the poor." Sometimes we foolishly make sport of such frugal friends. We forget that they are always able and eager to reach out hands full of good things needful for God's suffering poor. Once again, "She openeth her mouth with wisdom; and in her tongue is the law of kindness." Such "sweetness and light" issue from a heart overflowing with love for the God who is "most wonderfully kind."

> And on that cheek, and o'er that brow,
>   So soft, so calm, so eloquent,
> The smiles that win, the tints that glow
>   But tell of days in goodness spent,
> A mind at peace with all below,
>   A heart whose love is innocent![3]

---

[3][Lord Byron (George Gordon), "She Walks in Beauty (like the Night)," *The Oxford Book of English Verse 1250–1918*, new edition, ed. Arthur Quiller-Couch (New York, Toronto: Oxford University Press, 1939; [1]1900) #607, lines 13-18.]

The Influence of a Godly Wife

In Bible days the Hebrews believed in marriage. Rightly did they look upon it as the normal state of human beings here below. In it they found earth's nearest approach to heaven. By way of contrast think of the blight that falls upon many a home in days of war and reconstruction. Not only does war lead young folks to hasten or else postpone their wedding day; it also slays many a noble youth who would have gloried in being a husband and father. War likewise leaves unsought many a winsome maiden whom God must have meant to serve the common weal as a wife and mother in a Christian home.

Whether in war or peace, the woman who fears the Lord takes delight in being true to her marriage vows.

In plenty and in want;
in joy and in sorrow;
in sickness and in health;
as long as we both do live.

"The heart of her husband doth safely trust in her." Because she loves her God supremely, she is ever loyal to her husband. In every relation of their life together she wins the right to be called his helpmeet. Instead of adding to her husband's burdens, year after year she stands back of him as a sort of silent partner. "She will do him good and not evil all the days of his life." Through their love for each other the two of them grow daily more like their God.

Largely because of her unseen influence, the husband may be a power among his fellow men. If so, he becomes "known in the gates, when he sitteth among the elders of the land." Little does he or anyone else ever dream that the inspiration and the strength for his life of service come from God through the influence of a quiet woman. She believes in her beloved. She expects from him everything good and high. This motif prevails in the charming domestic drama by Sir James M. Barrie, *What Every Woman Knows*.[4] What does she know? She knows how to buckle the armor of her husband's heart so that he stands up day after day to win victories for the

-----

[4][James Matthew Barrie, *What Every Woman Knows* (New York: Scribner's, 1918).]

living God. Some such vision must have been glowing in the eyes of Wordsworth when he sang:

A perfect woman, nobly plann'd
To warn, to comfort, and command;
And yet a spirit still, and bright
With something of angelic light.[5]

By this time someone may be tempted to protest: "Your good woman seems to be busy and troubled about many things! Is she not a martyr to a mistaken sense of duty?" No, not from the biblical point of view. Her kind of love never counts the cost of doing good. If ever she were tempted to pity herself as a sort of household helper she might recall the old-time essay by William C. Gannett, "Blessed Be Drudgery":

[W]e have to go, and go, morning after morning, through rain, through shine, through tooth-ache, heart-ache to the appointed spot, and do the appointed work; because, and only because, we have to stick to that work through the eight or ten hours, long after rest would be so sweet; . . . because good temper must be kept with children, customers, neighbors, not seven, but seventy times seven times; because the besetting sin must be watched today, tomorrow, and the next day; in short, without much matter what our work be, . . . it is because and only because, of the rut, plot, grind, hum-drum in the work, that we at last get those self-foundations laid of which I spoke,—attention, promptness, accuracy, firmness, patience, self-denial, and the rest. . . . Then beyond all books, beyond all class-work at the school, beyond all special opportunities of what I call my "education," it is this drill and pressure of my daily task that is my great school master. My daily task, whatever it be, that is what mainly educates me. . . . Yet, fool that I am, this pressure of my daily task is the very thing that I so growl at as my "Drudgery"!. . .
. . . Blessed be Drudgery,—the secret of all culture![6]

---

[5][Wordsworth, "Perfect Woman," lines 27-30.]
[6][William Channing Gannett, "Blessed Be Drudgery" (orig. 1886), e.g., in *Blessed by* [*sic*] *Drudgery and Other Papers* (London: Bagster, 1916) 3, 9.]

The Praises of a Godly Mother

Most of all did the ancient Hebrews believe in the bearing of children. This belief also came from God. It still lies close to God's heart. Not only does he wish to be known as Father. He has likewise filled the mother heart with a love like his own. "As one who his mother comforteth, so will I comfort you" (Isaiah 66:13). Hence the noblest tribute any mortal can bestow on a woman in the home is to call her a godly mother. Such a tribute may be one of her chief rewards, both on earth and in glory.

"Her children arise up and call her blessed; her husband also, and he praiseth her." The rest of the poem tells what these loved ones ought to say while she is with them in the flesh. After her children are mature, and have little ones of their own, her sons and daughters should begin to appreciate their mother. They should delight to join with their father in voicing her praises as the uncrowned queen of the home. If they are wise they understand that their mother loves and trusts each of her children, that she prays and hopes for them one by one, and that she lives and toils for them all together. Indeed, she would gladly suffer and die to shield any of them from harm.

In Kentucky years ago such a saintly mother presided over a ranch of the Breckinridge clan. From that home went forth a group comprising the most illustrious sons of the Bluegrass State, if not of the entire South. A familiar legend says that after the four sons had become famous, each in a different sphere, they all came home to spend Christmas with their mother, then a widow. As they sat together around the family table one of them said to her playfully, "Mother, you and father were the noblest parents that growing boys could ever know and love. But don't you think you were too strict with us when we were small?"

"Robert," came the answer, also with a smile, "when you have reared four sons as fine as I have, you can begin telling me how to raise children." Well did she know that the family tree should be judged by the quality of its fruit.

Even the saintliest mother, however, cannot linger in the family circle forever. After she has gone home to her God, the children of her heart's love still rise up and call her blessed. Indeed, more than a few grown sons and daughters calmly accept their mother's devotion as long as she tarries with them in the flesh. At last, when she has lain down to sleep at the end of her days on earth, they find that they have had in their midst a dear one much like God in heaven. Some such discovery has led more than one worldly son or daughter to accept mother's Savior after she has gone home to rest. Perhaps this is what the apostle means by his unusual words about being "baptized for the dead" (1 Corinthians 15:29).

Once again I hear a protest. This one should be doubly welcome, for it comes from an aged mother, who has never spoken out in a meeting. Surely she has a right to be heard in the sanctuary! "Tell us," she whispers, "less about mothers and more about God." That is well spoken. God alone can be the source of all that is true and strong, all that is lovely and enduring, in the heart and life of any mother. Hence we should thank our God for letting his love and mercy shine out on the world through the windows of a home where she is more than a queen. Of such a dwelling place, full of light and life and love, LeBaron Russell Briggs teaches us to sing:

Thine is the strong and solemn glow,
Thine is the sweet abounding grace,
On her whose love, through weal and woe,
Lights her transcendent face.
Where hope is high and thought is free,
Where life is brave and death is true,
Where duty unrelenting leads
To tasks of pain forever new,
The heart that triumphs while it bleeds,
Mother, thy face we see.

This would be a fitting stage for a word of prayer. In it everyone should accept anew the mercies that come from God through mother's love. Afterward we all could sing a parting hymn. Then the minister would pronounce the benediction of God's light and peace. On the homeward way one after another might exclaim: "I am truly grateful for my mother and her undying love!"

All that has its worthy place, but still God requires more. God has no patience with sentimentality. How can he bless a man or a woman who receives but never shares? The Lord's standard for living in a home is clear: "Unto whomsoever much is given, of him much is required" (Luke 12:48). Here and now God wishes each of you to ask: "Am I worthy of my mother's love? Am I walking in her footsteps, even as she followed the Savior and Master?"

A Father's Failure

*O my son Absalom, my son, my son Absalom! Would God I had
died for thee, o Absalom, my son my son!*   (2 Samuel 18:33 KJV)

Here is an exceedingly bitter cry that even now tends to make our blood run
cold. There are tears upon it that have not been dried by the hot suns of the
centuries. Who is this that is giving way to such an abandon of grief? Surely
it must be some mother perchance, whose empty arms are aching for the
boy that she had loved and lost. No, that is not the case. This is not the wail
of a woman, but of a man; not of a mother, but of a father. It is King David
breaking his heart over what he regards as the greatest failure of his life.

Wherein has David failed? Surely his failure is not full-orbed. In many
respects he has been vastly successful. The story of his thrilling career reads
like a romance. He came up from the ranks. Once he was only a shepherd
lad with no great standing even in his own family. But he had a mind that
was as brilliant as the kiss of sunlight upon clear water. He was possessed
of a dauntless courage. If tradition is correct, he had the genius of a poet.
While at his worst he was a great sinner, at his best he was a great saint.
Then he was vastly attractive. Upon all with whom he came into contact he
cast a spell that was all but irresistible. Then, too, he was a practical man of
affairs with his feet firmly fixed upon the ground. He was a many-sided
man, eminently fitted by nature to make good in any situation.

And make good he did. He climbed by rapid strides till he became king,
not by right of birth, but by right of ability. As king he served his people
well. He proved himself at once a great soldier and a great statesman. He
soon succeeded in welding a few scattered, quarreling tribes into a
compactly organized nation. He made a success financially. Much of the
vast wealth that went into the building of the temple came through his
hands. In fact so wisely did he reign that his people, throughout their
subsequent history, looked back to his day as a Golden Age of Israel. Had
he lived in our day we should doubtless have written a book about him
entitled "From Shepherd's Tent to King's Palace." This book would
certainly have found a place in "The Success Series" and would have
become a best seller.

In what, then, did this greatly successful man fail? He failed as a father.
As a result of that failure, the body of his handsome, gifted, and favorite son
became a crushed wreck in a pit in the wilderness. Therefore, while others

would surely have been thrilled by the reading of David's biography, I seriously doubt if he himself would have read it with any real satisfaction. The very brilliance of his success in certain directions must have served to give only the greater emphasis to his failure in another. As he read he would have realized that his victories had been many and worthy. He had certainly won a secure place in the hearts of his people. But in spite of all this, the book would have left him cold. He would have been made to feel that, after all, he had majored on minors, and that his success, though very real, had been bought as too great a price.

And this is the record of so many men who are otherwise successful. I have in mind a certain gentleman who out of small beginnings succeeded in building a fortune of several millions. His brilliant success as a financier blazoned his name to the world and made him at once an object of envy and of honor. But his wealth, I am told by one who knew him well, became a weight instead of wings. It caught and held him as a piece of flypaper catches and holds a fly. In his efforts to be free, he was at times little better than a madman. Of course he had little or no time for his family. His boys grew into soft and pulpy manhood. They were far less suited to cope with their situation than their hard-working father had been to cope with his. When he died, his gold seemed to sweep over them a bit like an avalanche. They were completely swamped by their unearned wealth. Thus their father, while providing himself a conspicuous success in the building of a future, proved himself a yet more conspicuous failure in the building of men.

A few years ago, at a state fair, a crowd was gathered about a prize hog. That hog was about all that a hog could be. His hair was parted in the middle and nicely combed. His hoofs were manicured in such a fashion as to have roused the envy of a movie star. Everybody who saw that hog realized that the man who raised him knew his business. Now, the boy who was set to look after this hog seemed to have been chosen as a foil to further emphasize the hog's perfection. He was a little wizen-faced, hollow-chested, hatchet-headed fellow who seemed bent upon burning up all the cigarettes in the world, and that as quickly as possible. He would not have walked a mile, I dare say, for his favorite brand, for he did not seem to have strength enough. He had too evidently found his unlucky strike. But the most startling feet about the whole situation was this: the father of the boy and the owner of the hog was the same man. In the hog business this father was a huge success. In the boy business he was an utter failure. And in spite of his vast abilities this also was one of the tragedies of the life of David.

Why Was David's Heart So Completely Broken?

First, it was broken because of his deep and tender love for the son that he had lost. This I say in spite of the fact that he was only a father. Fathers are not generally credited with doing much loving, you know. They are not supposed greatly to care. To be convinced that this is the common view, it is only necessary to contrast the celebration of Mother's Day with that of Father's Day. On the former we come together in large numbers. We come with our largest handkerchiefs, for the atmosphere is redolent of sentiment, and we are ready at the slightest provocation to burst into tears. On Father's Day we still bring our handkerchiefs, but we use them to stifle our yawns rather than to dry our tears. However, unlike the Master though Dad may be in other respects, he is at least like him in this: he has made himself of no reputation!

Now, this lack of popularity is, of course, in part his own fault, but it is not altogether so. In my opinion it is at once unfortunate and unfair, as another has suggested, that a golden halo for mother is altogether fitting. It blesses both us who give and she who receives. But I believe also that it would be good, if we could find it in our hearts to do so, to give a little "halo" to father now and then. It might serve to encourage him to do better. Then I ask it in the name of fair play. As I think of my own mother, I think of one who was both funny and serious, with never a thought of herself. As I think of my father, I think of one who was more rugged and stern, but whose unselfish devotion to his own could no more be doubted than hers. David was a father but his heart is broken over the loss of his boy.

Second, David is crushed because his loss is without remedy. There are some mistakes we can correct. Having blundered, we may promise ourselves to do better next time. But in many instances there is no next time. That is the tragic note in that "exceeding bitter cry" of Esau. He found no way of undoing the past. He could not get back into yesterday and place in his hands again the tremendous opportunities that were his own life's bright morning long ago. What was done could never be undone. It is this realization that made the grief of David all the more bitter. He was facing the fact that of the things that have no next time, one, at least, is the rearing of a son. How many things he felt he could do for Absalom were he only a little boy again. But that can never be. Therefore, there is the agony of utter hopelessness in his cry, "O my son Absalom, O my son Absalom. Would I had died for thee."

Third, the note of supreme bitterness in the sorrow of David, that which brought his grief to its tragic climax, was the haunting fear that the boy that he had lost hopelessly he had also lost needlessly. He had lost him when he might have saved him. "Had I only been a better father to him, had I only acted differently," he kept telling his tortured soul, "then he would be with me now instead of yonder in the pit, under the stones. I have lost him and it's all my fault." This was the nagging fear that became a conviction that he could not shake off. It was a conviction that bit like a serpent and stung like an adder. His loss would have been hard enough if he could have persuaded himself that he had done his best. But this he could not do. His hell was that such a persuasion was impossible.

One day a Texas farmer was in the field plowing cotton. With him were his two small boys. He looked up from his task to see a large dog coming toward them. This dog was snapping at the cotton stalks and the farmer realized that he was mad. At once he put himself between his boys and the dog. He told them to run for refuge to a nearby cotton bin, while he kept the dog away. The boys made good their escape. Not so the father. He was forced to fight the dog with no weapon but his pocketknife. As a result he was bitten from his face to his feet. Medical science could do nothing for him. But during his lucid intervals, as death crept upon him, he would look into the face of his wife with a smile and say, "Don't you worry about me. I saved our boys." And he went out to meet God unafraid. I think he could have done so, even if the boys had died with him, seeing that he did his best. But to lose when we might have done better, that is "sorrow's crown of sorrow." And that was the pathetic plight of David. He had lost his son and lost him hopelessly and needlessly.

How Did David Come to Make This Terrible Failure?

He did not do so, I am sure, because Absalom was born a traitor. He was born with a capacity for treachery, but he was also born with a capacity for faithfulness and loyalty. "What manner of child shall this be?" asked the group that stood about the cradle of John the Baptist. Is there any sure answer to such a question? The Catholic Church has always believed that there is. As it looks into the face of a little child, it says without hesitation, "This child will be a Catholic." The Jews believe that there is an answer to that question. As they look into the face of a baby, they do not hesitate to say, "This child will be a Jew." But the Protestants are often far less sure. That is one of our chief weaknesses. Too often we answer, "The Lord only knows," and then we hurry about our business or pleasure. Yet both the

Scriptures and experience teach that if we train a child in the way that he shall go, when he is old, he will not depart from it.

If, then, David did not fail because failure was inevitable, why did he fail? There are, I think, two outstanding reasons.

First, he failed because he shifted the responsibility for the care of his son onto the shoulders of others instead of taking it upon himself. What he did in this last scene is, I think, typical of his entire relationship to Absalom. When his soldiers were going out to battle, a battle that was to determine whether he himself was to keep his crown and his life, it was not of these that he was thinking. He was thinking only of his loved and treacherous son. "Deal gently for my sake," he told his officers in the presence of his army. "Deal gently, for my sake, with the young man Absalom." But when the army had marched out of sight, he was doubtless very uneasy, "My officers are good and loyal men," he probably kept telling himself, "still I am greatly afraid for my son. I should have gone myself. Yes, at all costs I should have made the safety of my boy a personal matter."

But who was that coming across the plain? It was a messenger. The king was all solicitude but his anxiety was only for his son. "Victory," the messenger shouts through panting lips. But the father has no ear for such a message. There is but one question: "Is the young man Absalom safe?" The first messenger did not have the heart to tell, but yonder came another. "Victory!" he shouted also. But David asked that same eager, anxious question: "Is the young man Absalom safe?" Then came the tragic answer and David is a broken old man. "O my son, Absalom," he sobbed, "I am so sorry now that I did not go out even at the cost of my life. Better a million times that I should be lying under the stones than you."

What David did in this instance he had done through the years. It is true that he had a good excuse for his conduct. We are in no sense disposed to judge him harshly. He had been a man of many cares. He had been burdened by matters of state. Naturally he had not had much time for his children. But we cannot shut our eyes to the pathos of it all, for he never really got acquainted with Absalom, never gained his confidence, never won his heart. In his younger years, when he had a broken bow, Absalom never thought of going to his father about it. Nor did he think of doing so in later years when he had a broken heart. Father and son were both most fascinating but they never became friends. Yet David gave him everything except himself. But failing to give himself, he failed altogether. Thus he lost a treasure far more priceless than his crown.

How David would have envied the humble father of whom his son could say:

He's the best thing, daddy is,
When he ain't got the rheumatiz,
Gives me pennies and good advice,
'Bout keeping clean and being nice,
Saying please, and don't deceive,
Handkerchief instead of sleeve.
Seems just like 'at daddy knew,
He was once a small boy, too,
Second table for him, I spec,
With nothing but the chicken neck.
Anyhow he always says,
Give the kid the best there is.
And when Ma sends me off to bed,
He always takes the light ahead,
And holds my hand and talks maybe,
About things that used to be,
When he and uncle were little boys,
And all about their games and toys,
When am I gonner be, Gee whiz,
I'm gonner be like daddy is,
I'd rather be like him, I jing,
Than president or anything.
He's like Ma says angels is
When he ain't got the rheumatiz.

But David was too busy. Like so many today he "passed the buck," lost his boy, and broke his own heart.

The second reason for David's failure was his bad example. There was a time, after he had become a father, that he allowed himself a most tragic visit to the far country. He became a prodigal. In utter disregard to his obligations to others, he took a woman to whom he had no right. Later he murdered her husband to conceal his crime. No wonder that when his oldest son wanted a woman for himself, he took her ruthlessly, even though she was his half-sister. Had not his father set him the example? And that father, having done so, dared not punish his brutal son. Thus Absalom felt called upon to take vengeance into his own hands and punish his brother. All this brought an ever-widening chasm between himself and his father until it ended in utter tragedy. No wonder, therefore, that David felt, and rightly so, that he had the blood of his ruined boy on his own hands. He had employed two most effective methods of destruction, a bad example and neglect.

But, you answer, was not David a good man? Yes, David repented of his terrible sin and God in his mercy forgave him. But, while David's repentance brought him personal salvation, it did not bring salvation to his wayward boy. David made one excursion into the far country, and Absalom followed his steps; but when David came back, so far as this son was concerned, he came back alone. That is a tragedy that has happened times without number. Years ago I had a neighbor who was the father of a large family. He was a drinking man, though not a drunkard. He was friendly toward religion, though he seldom went to church. But when he was between fifty and sixty years of age, he was soundly and happily converted. How hard he tried to atone for his wasted years. How eager he was to reach his children, all of whom had now grown to manhood and womanhood. I have seen him stand up in the church to read a bit, only to burst into tears. But his children were not softened by these tears; they were only shamed by them. They went with him into the far country, but the poor broken father came back alone. May God save us from such a tragedy. Let parents in the fear of God take the responsibility for the welfare of their children upon themselves.

Part 7

Holy Days and Holidays

The Incarnation

Who, being in the form of God, counted it not a prize to be on an equality with God, but emptied himself, taking the form of a servant, being made in the likeness of men. (Philippians 2:6 ERV)

There is only one thing a preacher can possibly speak about this morning and that is the wonderful and blessed event which this Sunday celebrates. This is the day that the Christian church observes as the birthday of Jesus Christ. It does not matter whether this was the actual day of his nativity or not. He may have been born not in December but in April. Kings have power to fix their own official birthdays. And this is the official birthday of our glorious and blessed king. Inspiring our songs, prompting our rejoicing, is the great historic fact that nineteen centuries ago "Christ was born in Bethlehem." I get a little jealous at Christmas time lest in our many reasons for happiness and gaiety we should forget or ignore the supreme reason of all.

There were Christmas festivals in existence before Christ came, though they did not bear that name. There was the great Yule feast of the Norsemen extending from the 25th of December to the 6th of January, at which time with feasting and revelry they celebrated the turn of the year and the promise of new life and activity in nature. There was the festival of the Saturnalia in Rome lasting for six or seven days at the close of December, at which people were accustomed to send presents to one another, during which it was impious to begin a war or execute a criminal; for one day at any rate the slave became a free man and sat at table while his master served him. What the church did was to lay hold of these ancient festivals with their many gracious customs and convert what was often a riot of revelry into a time of sacred and holy joy by definitely associating them with the celebration of the birth of Christ.

Some of the customs of those old primitive festivals are still embedded in our Christmas feastings, our cards, our presents, our holidays, and our family parties. I am not criticizing these things. Only a fool would dream of criticizing them. They are a part and a very real part of the joy of this happy season. The most precious thing in life, next to the love of God, is the love and affection of our fellows. And we do well to rejoice in the evidences of these which this season brings. They warm the heart and add enormously to our Christmas gladness. But I get a little jealous sometimes lest these purely human causes of rejoicing should wholly absorb and possess our minds, lest Christmas should become to us a season of family gatherings and presents and parties and nothing more. For there is a far deeper and richer element in the gladness of Christmas then any of these things can supply. So long as we identify Christmas simply with our gaieties (however welcome and altogether delightful they may be) we are living in the pre-Christian time of the Saturnalia and Yuletide. What makes Christmas Christmas, what supplies to Christmas its characteristic joy is this: that we remember today that in the person of Jesus, God entered human life.

There never was a birth like the birth of Jesus. I am not now thinking of the marvelous accompaniments of that birth—the singing of the angels and the adoring worship of the shepherds. What I am thinking of is this—the birth in Bethlehem was not the beginning of the life of Jesus. That is what differentiates it from every birth. As for the rest of us, the hour of our birth marks the beginning of our individual life. But Jesus lived before Bethlehem. He was not so much "born"; he "came." His birth was an Advent. That is the truth my text emphasizes. I am not going to discuss in detail the expressions the apostle uses—though every one of them would repay study—I have quoted it simply for the central truth it propounds, namely, that Jesus lived in glory with his Father before he was born in Bethlehem, but that he did not think his equality with God a thing to be snatched at and clung to, but "emptied himself" and taking the form of a servant, was make in the likeness of men. The birth was not a simple birth; it was an incarnation. It was the deliberate and willing act of the Eternal Son. He "took hold" of the seed of Abraham. In the babe then born the coequal Son submitted to the conditions of space and time and God became Emmanuel, God with us.

The coming of God's Son caused no ripple of excitement in the world into which he came. With the exception of a few humble shepherds nobody in Palestine knew that anything extraordinary was happening. For nothing could have been simpler, humbler, more unostentatious than the manner in which he came. When an heir to the throne of Britain is expected, great officers of state wait in the palace for the first announcement of his birth and the whole population stands on the tiptoe of expectancy. But when God's Son was born no one watched or waited for his coming. He was born into an unconcerned world. A poor peasant woman with her hour close upon her reached Bethlehem and because there was not room in the inn she brought forth her first son and cradled him amongst the beasts of the stall.

Who could be expected to notice so lowly and insignificant an event as that? Herod in his palace knew nothing of it. The priests in Jerusalem knew nothing of it. Caesar, the master of the world away yonder in Rome, though before that child's power the empire was one day to yield, knew nothing of it. And yet the coming of that little child, so lowly, so humble, so unostentatious, was the most stupendous event in the history of the world.

It is the most stupendous event from the point of view of its consequences for the world's life. Think of the great and critical events in the world's history—those great migrations in the dim and distant years of far antiquity, Thermopyle and Salamis when the tide of Eastern invasion was rolled back from Europe, the conquests of Alexander, the establishment of the Roman Empire and its subsequent fall, the emergence of the Mohammedan power and its conquest of Eastern Europe—they were mighty events, but they pale in significance and hide their diminished heads by the side of this event of the birth of Mary's little child. For that child, as someone has said, lifted the world from its hinges and changed the current of history. It has been his world ever since, as we ourselves testify when we date our years from the year of his birth.

But the greatest thing about that birth is not that it changed the current of history; the greatest thing about it is that in it the Eternal Son was made in human likeness. God entered into human life. The invisible God took form. The unknown God revealed himself. He tabernacled among people so that they beheld his glory. It is this that makes the birth at Bethlehem the most stupendous event in the world's history, the great miracle of all time. It is not only the most stupendous event but also the most gracious, the most comforting, and the most uplifting. It is from the contemplation of this side of Christmas, its divine side, if I may so phrase it, that the deepest joys arise and the most rapturous songs are inspired. The knowledge that people want most to acquire is the knowledge of God. They want to know how God feels towards them. They know that God is. Atheism is unnatural. Human beings in the depths of their being are incorrigibly religious. They know there is a Supreme Being with whom they have to do and that their ultimate happiness depends on the attitude of that great Being toward them. They saw the activities of God in nature, but nature left them in doubt as to his character. They saw his operations on the field of history, but history could give them no sure answer. Nature and history left people still wondering whether God was a good God and whether his attitude towards them was one of helpfulness and love. And there was no real peace for people so long as god was an unknown quantity, so long as the highest altar they could raise was an altar to the unknown God.

"The proper study of mankind is man," sang an English poet. But long before him the Greek sage had said very much the same thing when he gave this counsel: "Know thyself." But there is no hope or comfort in the knowledge of oneself. The inward look brings us no sort of cheer. Our hearts, when we look within, condemn us. "Vile and full of sin, we are." And besides, human beings cannot be limited to the task of self-scrutiny. They have eternity in their hearts and they are made for God. It is with God and not simply with themselves that they have to do and they know it.

That is why I say again that the knowledge people desire most, the knowledge that will make all the difference between misery and joy, is the knowledge of God. Human beings want to know what God is like. This God whose movements they can discern, whose activities they can behold, whose presence they can feel—is he a good God? Is love at the heart of these things? That is the crucial question and you can hear it asked, as Dr. Mackintosh says, "in the undertones of the world's literature as well as in those desperate experiments of supplication of which the lower religions are full." And the answer to that crucial, agonizing, torturing question is given in the Christmas fact. God is like Jesus Christ. God is in Jesus Christ. In Jesus we see God himself under the limitations of space and time. God was not content to send a sympathetic message to people or to appear amongst them by deputy—he had done all that already in the prophets—but he came himself in the person of his Son. And by coming he has made us quite sure that his name and nature is love, uttermost love, redeeming love, love so deep that to accomplish his redeeming work he stooped to shame and death.

That is the Christmas gospel. The God whose character nature and history leave doubtful is revealed to us as the Father in Christ. We know now that back of all the varied experiences of human life there lies an infinite love, for God and Christ are one thing.

Now that is a tremendous gospel, if it is true. But can we believe it? Can we believe that in the child Jesus, God entered human life? Can we really believe that God became a man? The very idea of Incarnation seems almost incredible and gives rise to the sorts of questions in which the wistful doubts of people express themselves. "Wistful doubts" I call them because people would like to believe it. It would make all the difference to them if they could heartily believe it. But the questions they ask are questions like these: Is an incarnation possible? If it is possible, is it likely? If it is likely, did it actually take place in Jesus? Will you let me on this Christmas

Sunday glance briefly at those questions in which the doubts and hesitations of people express themselves and see whether a satisfactory answer can be given?

Is Incarnation Possible?

Is incarnation possible? I answer, unhesitatingly, Yes. "Scripture knows nothing," says Dr. Kilpatrick, "of such disparity between the divine and human natures as to make the idea of incarnation an intellectual impossibility." Of course, it is impossible for a person completely to express himself in a thing or a creature essentially different and disparate. An artist can put his mind into his work but he cannot put his total self into it. God can put his mind into the universe of created things so that the heavens shall declare his glory and the firmament show forth his handiwork. But God cannot fully reveal himself in suns and stars because the ultimate truth about God is not power and wisdom but holiness and love.

God can, however, express himself in a being possessed of moral personality like his own. And such is humanity, according to the biblical account of him: "And God said, Let us make man in our image, after our likeness. . . . So God created man in his own image, in the image of God created he him; male and female created he them." That is what differentiates human beings from every other thing and creature in the universe: human beings are made in the image of God. That word "image" must not be interpreted of visible and external form; the real likeness between God and humans is that both possess moral personality. A human being is a thinking, willing, moral being as God himself is, so that union between the two ceases to be impossible. As a matter of fact, God dwells in conscience, for instance, in every person. Seeing that he partially inhabits all people, there is no reason in the nature of things why he should not completely inhabit some chosen one.

If the objection is raised that it is impossible for the infinite God to incarnate himself in a finite being, let it be freely conceded that such incarnation involves self-limitation or what Paul calls "self-emptying." When the Eternal Son entered human life he laid his divine glories by. Omniscience, omnipotence, omnipresence—those qualities which set forth the infinitude of God—he divested himself of them all. But again I say that the real essence of God's nature is his holiness and his love. It is in these things and not in those attributes of immensity that the ultimate secret of his personality is to be found. And these things could be and were expressed within the limits of human life.

"It is as absurd," someone may say, "to think that God can become incarnate and express himself in human life, as it would be to say that the ocean can be contained in a tiny cup." Well, it would be absurd to suggest that the ocean in its immensity—Atlantic, Pacific, Artic Oceans and multitudinous seas—could be contained in a cup. But the ocean in its nature can be contained in a cup. The sea is the same sea everywhere. You take a cupful of water on Jacksonville Beach and you know the nature of the sea on the other side of the world. The sea is there in that cup. You know the whole sea when you know that cupful. And although the immensity and infinity of God cannot be expressed in human life, his nature can. The infinities of God are not in Jesus, but his nature is. And we know God in every part of his nature when we know him in Jesus. In those infinities and immensities that are beyond our grasp, he is still perfect holiness and measureless redeeming love.

Is Incarnation Likely?

I pass on now to the second question. Admitting that incarnation is theoretically possible, is it likely? Again without hesitation I answer, Yes. It is likely on a double ground, one human and one divine. It is likely on a human ground. The expectation of an incarnation was widespread, not to say universal. I know that some people use the fact that we find incarnation stories in other religions as an argument against the reality of God's incarnation in Jesus. They quote the avatars of Vishnu in Hinduism, his tenfold incarnation, and the stories of Greek mythology about the appearances of the gods in the likeness of men, and the implication suggested is that all these incarnations stand on very much the same plane—they have no more real substance than myths or legends or fairy tales.

But looked at soberly, these widespread stories of incarnation are not an argument against the real incarnation of God in Jesus but an argument for it. For they speak of a general hunger for the appearance of God in human form. They constitute no proof that a real incarnation did not come at last; they rather suggest that such a real incarnation must take place, unless the deepest instincts and the desires of the human soul are to be written down as deceptive and false. Did God, who over against the eye provided a world of beauty to be seen and over against the ear a world of glorious sound to be heard and over against the instinct of love human beings to be loved—did he plant these deepest cravings of the soul within us simply to mock and torture us? Let those who wish to believe that believe it. I believe that every craving prophesy is its own fulfillment. "If

we are so made," says Mr. Chesterton, "that a Son of God must deliver us,
is it odd that Patagonians should dream of a Son of God?"[1] No, it is not odd.
It is the most natural thing in the world. In these so-called "pagan Christs"
I see just evidence of the world's hunger for the real Christ. The answer to
the world's hunger for God came when Christ was born in Bethlehem.

The incarnation is likely from the divine side too, for if humanity wants
God, God wants humanity. Human beings are God's children. He created
them to be the object of his love. Do you think that God could remain dumb
and hold himself aloof when he saw these human children of his falling into
danger and error and sin? Do you think he could refrain from revealing
himself when he saw his children living in fear and misery just because they
were ignorant of his real nature? There came a point in Joseph's dealings
with his brethren when he could no longer contain himself. It cut him to the
quick to see these brothers cowering before him in sheer terror. So to put an
end to their fears and dreads he revealed himself, crying, "I am Joseph, your
brother!" It cut God to the quick to see his children plunged into misery and
despair all for lack of really knowing him. So at the earliest moment he
revealed himself to them in his Son. Love lay behind the birth at Bethlehem.
"God so loved the world that he gave his only begotten Son."

I look at humanity, hungering for a true knowledge of God, and I
conclude that unless the deepest instincts and impulses of the soul are to be
dismissed as lies, incarnation is likely. I think of God, loving his human
children, and I know that incarnation is not only likely; it is inevitable.

Did Incarnation Take Place?

I come now to the third question. Assuming that incarnation is possible
and likely, did it actually take place in Jesus? Again, I personally have no
hesitation in answering yes – though quite possibly my assurance will not
bring assurance to you. For you cannot demonstrate the true Deity of Christ
like you can demonstrate a theorem of Euclid. The incarnation does not
admit of mathematical proof. It is a spiritual fact that can only be spiritually
discerned. But there are three lines of evidence which I would press upon
our consideration.

There is first the evidence of what Jesus was in himself. On the
testimony of those who lived nearest to him, he was "holy, harmless,

---

[1][G. K. Chesterton, "Christianity and Rationalism," in *The Religious Doubts
of Democracy*, ed. George Haw (London: Macmillan, 1904).]

undefiled, separate from sinners. . . . Who did no sin, neither was guile found in his mouth" (Hebrews 7:26; 1 Peter 2:22). Peter, James, John, Matthew lived in closest intimacy with him. It is always our intimates who know our faults. In public we maintain a certain hold of ourselves. But in the privacy of our own homes we relax and those who live with us see our weaknesses only too plainly. But these men who shared Christ's privacy not only saw no weakness or defect but gradually became so impressed by his goodness and greatness that, stern monotheists as they were, they came to worship him as God. He is never simply Jesus to them; he is Lord and Christ. More remarkable still, Jesus had no conviction of sin himself. It is ever the best people who are more conscious of failure. But Jesus had no such sense. On the contrary, he knew himself to be in the closest communion with God. He asserted for himself an unshared relationship with God. Now, what are you to make of this absolutely sinless person? If he was only a man, why has there never been another like him? Can we account for him in any other way than by saying he was the Son of God?

There is second the evidence of history. What I mean is this: there is the immense and unparalleled influence that Christ has had on the after history of the world. The world in which we live is his world. His birth was the great watershed of history. The modern world began with his birth. It is his new creation. It is *Anno Domini*, the year of our Lord. No other person in history has exercised an influence in any way comparable to his. We talk about great people ruling us from their graves. But the very phrase suggests their rule is a shadowy and insubstantial thing. It is from their graves as pale ghosts, as vague and dim memories, that they rule and influence us. But Jesus is a living energy. He is a presence. We talk of certain nations in the world as "the Great Powers." But the greatest power is Jesus. What are you to say of him, this person who rules the world, and rules it to redeem it, and who is changing it before our very eyes? To believe that God was in Christ is to give an adequate explanation; to say Jesus was a man who lived and died 2,000 years ago is to present yourself with an unexplainable problem.

And there is finally the evidence of experience. I know one person's experience will not avail for another, but the testimony of experience is to be heeded by us all. And here is the testimony of the best and noblest of our race: that Christ has done God's work in them and upon them. He has really given them, for instance, the forgiveness of sins, and only God can do that. He has really given them victorious power. He has really bestowed upon them eternal life and in their most sacred moments God and Christ cease to be two and become merged into one. He has done all that for some of us.

What can we say of him who has given us forgiveness, power, and life, save that he is God? From the days of the apostles down to these days of ours there is a multitude which no man can number who have obtained from him and through him all that is meant by salvation. He has loosed them from their sins and made them to be kings and priests unto God. They worship and adore him because of what he has done in them and for them. The deity of Christ is not a doctrine invented by the theologians and foisted upon the church; it is simply the expression of people that declares that Jesus is God.

And that experience may be ours. We have but to let Christ have his way with us, to let him work his gracious will upon us, and he will demonstrate his own divinity. He will reconcile us to God, take our sins away, fill us with a new power and peace, until we shall join in the old song "Come and behold him Christ the Lord."

The Empty Tomb

Behold, the place where they laid him!   (Mark 16:6)

It was on the day before the Sabbath that the crucifixion took place and that particular Sabbath was, as John says, "A high day." It was because the Jews did not want the Sabbath to be shamed by the sight of three writhing victims hanging on their crosses just outside the walls that they came to Pilate with the request that their legs should be broken and so have an end put to their miseries. There was no need to inflict that last indignity upon Jesus, for he was already dead. At the ninth hour, that is about three o'clock in the afternoon, he cried with a loud voice, "Father, into thy hands I commend my spirit" and having said this he gave up the ghost. Now it must be remembered that the Jewish Sabbath began at six o'clock on Friday evening. Therefore, all the preparations for Christ's funeral had to be crowded into a space of something short of three hours. First, Joseph had to go to Pilate and beg permission to care for the body of Jesus, and if official ways then were anything like official ways are now, that took some time. Then the new tomb in the garden had to be readied and the precious body had to be taken down from the cross. It was a hurried funeral. All had to be carried through before six o'clock and as a result the friends of Jesus were not able to pay the usual tributes of respect and love to their dear dead.

That Sabbath between the crucifixion and the resurrection was a heartbroken sort of Sabbath for the disciples. They hadn't believed that Jesus could die, so the cross, when it came, was a shattering blow not simply to their affections but to their faith. They were perhaps too stunned to think, but one thing that tragic cross made plain: that Jesus could not be the Messiah, and that in attaching themselves to him they had made a calamitous mistake. They loved Jesus still—they couldn't help doing that—but they believed that the cross had put an end to his cause. It was now for them a case of trying to piece together again the broken ends of their lives.

The women who loved Jesus and had followed him shared in that despair. They too felt that one who had hung upon the accursed tree could not be the Messiah. But disappointed though they were, with all their bright hopes falsified, they still cherished a deep and devoted love for Jesus. In spite of the shame of the cross, he was to them the altogether lovely. And it added to the bitterness of the sorrow of these women on that desolate Sabbath that they had been able to do nothing for their Lord's body. So as soon as the Sabbath was past, again when six o'clock in the evening came, they set about preparing spices in order to make up for what was omitted because of the hurry of the funeral. They prepared these spices overnight and then very early on the morning of the first day of the week, at sunrise, they made their way to the tomb.

On the way they worried themselves about the great stone with which the mouth of the tomb was closed. It was too big and massive for them to move and they wondered who would roll it away for them. But on they went nevertheless. They didn't turn back to call Peter or John or Thomas or some other of the men. They went on trusting that they would find someone in the garden to help them out of that difficulty. But when they actually got to that corner in Joseph's garden where the tomb was situated they found that their worry was quite needless, as worry so often is. For the stone, exceeding great as it was, was already rolled back. Then going right up to the tomb they saw not the body of Jesus but a white robed angel. They were amazed, bewildered, and thunderstruck. To them the angel said, "Be not amazed: ye seek Jesus, the Nazarene, who hath been crucified." He left them in no doubt that he knew whom they were seeking; notice the detail of the identification: "Jesus, the Nazarene, who hath been crucified." "He is risen," the angel added, "he is not here. Behold, the place where they laid him!"

"Behold the place!"—that was all there was to see. There was no Jesus there. But it was the place where they had laid him, for there were the discarded grave clothes and that hundred pound weight of myrrh and aloes which Nicodemus had brought, a tardy declaration of his love. But there was nothing else. If they expected, as they certainly did, to find in the tomb the body of their Lord bearing upon it the signs of the fury and malice of the priests—the brow all torn and mangled by the thorny crown, the hands and feet pierced by the nails, that spent and broken body which had been nailed to the cross—I say, if they came expecting that, they were disappointed. For it wasn't there.

Some years ago I paid a visit to a cemetery located on one of the great battlefields of the Civil War. I saw those places whose names are familiar to us all because of the deeds of valor associated with them. I could see in imagination the flash and roar of the guns and the scream of agonized and tortured men. But the day I visited the place, there was scarcely a trace left of the ruin and ravage of war. There were no ghastly sights to lacerate the feelings, there were no shattered buildings, no great shell holes, no bodies of broken men. It was a peaceful countryside I saw, with tilled fields and neat houses, with children playing in the yards and roads and a blue sky smiling down upon it. The voice of the lark was heard caroling the coming of spring. If I had gone there expecting to see gruesome reminders of war and its havoc, I was disappointed. All I saw was just "the place," the place where the long-drawn agony had been endured. It was much like that with these women. If they had come expecting to find that body bearing still the marks of the scourging and the cross, they were disappointed. There was no body for them to see. The grave in Joseph's garden was empty. All the angel could show them was "the place." "Behold," he said, "the place where they laid him!"

The Empty Tomb

"The place" was an empty place! The empty place was the reason the disciples began to realize that something stupendous had happened on the morning of the third day. The women found the grave empty. I like to picture the swift change of feeling that swept over that little band of disciples on that first Easter day. It opened for them in gloom and grief; all they could do was to weep over a dead Jesus. The grief changed into a cold fear when the women saw the empty grave; they thought that even the body of Jesus had not been allowed to rest in peace. The fear passed into bewilderment and an incredulous kind of amazement when they heard the angel say that he was risen. Finally the amazement passed into rapturous joy when they came face to face with the living Lord himself. But, it is safe to say, the disciples could never have believed in a real resurrection had they not first found the grave empty.

Many modern lives of Christ finish at the crucifixion. If they have a concluding chapter on some such subject as "What happened afterwards?" its purport generally is that nothing happened at all except, as a recent writer put it, "an inexplicable access of faith in Jesus as being actually alive." That is where Matthew Arnold ends—at the grave. You remember his familiar stanza:

Now he is dead! Far hence he lies,
In the lorn Syrian town;

And on his grave, with shining eyes,
The Syrian stars look down.[1]

But if that were true, if these women had found their Lord's body in the
tomb, there would have been no Christian faith and there would have been
no Christian church. The whole course of the world's history would have
been different. If the body of Jesus had been found in the grave, it is safe to
say that in a few days these disciples would have been scattered to their
homes and no more would have been heard of Jesus; his name would have
passed out of the minds of people as Anatole France makes it to have passed
out of Pilate's memory.

Something stupendous happened on the morning of the third day and
that something was neither more nor less than the resurrection of Jesus. The
resurrection of Jesus I say, not merely his spiritual survival but his bodily
resurrection. Dr. Denney bluntly says that if we cannot speak of a bodily
resurrection we should not speak of a resurrection at all.[2] No doubt our
Lord's body had undergone some strange transcendental change, but that
does not affect the central truth, that it was the full Jesus in his total
personality who rose again from the dead. Scholars and thinkers admit that
something tremendous happened on the morning of the third day, because
the change in the disciples and the existence of the Christian church need
accounting for. But the modern tendency is to limit the resurrection to
spiritual survival and to account for the change in the disciples by
explaining the appearances of the risen Lord as subjective experiences.

But if that is true, what became of Christ's body? When we come to
think of the body of Jesus we have only two alternatives. Either there was
a full resurrection as the New Testament says there was or somebody must
have rifled the tomb and taken Christ's body away. Who could have taken
the body of our Lord? Again, there are only two alternatives. Either His
friends must have taken it or His enemies must have done so. Both of these
alternatives land us in insurmountable difficulties.

---

[1][Matthew Arnold, "Obermann Once More," in *New Poems* (London:
Macmillan, 1867; "reprint of the first edition," Garden City NY: Dolphin Books,
Doubleday, 1961).]

[2][James Denney, "The Historical Basis of the Christian Faith: The Resurrection
of Jesus," in *Jesus and the Gospel: Christianity Justified in the Mind of Christ*
(New York: Eaton & Mains; Cincinnati: Jennings &b Graham, 1908) 102.]

Let us suppose that the disciples came by night and stole the body. That commits us to the impossible position that in a few days the apostles were preaching in Jerusalem the resurrection of Jesus and risking prison and death because they persisted in preaching it while all the while they knew it to be false because they had the dead body of Jesus on their hands. Let us suppose that the enemies of Jesus had taken his body. That lands us in the equally impossible position of finding the apostles preaching the resurrection in Jerusalem when the priests could have put an end to their preaching once and for all and scattered the growing church into fragments by just producing the body or declaring that they had it. Either alternative is unthinkable. It is infinitely simpler to believe that on the morning of the third day the tomb was found empty because Jesus had really risen again. Nothing but a complete resurrection and an empty tomb could have enabled the disciples to recover their faith in Jesus as the victorious Messiah and the Prince of Life they believed him to be.

All Graves Are Empty

The grave of Jesus is typical of ours. He is the first fruits of them that slept. What happened to him is also what happens to every one who is a Christian. Every person in the world who is in union with him and who possesses his redeeming grace is victorious over the grave. Jesus came back from the other side of the grave not simply to make his disciples realize that he was alive and to open their eyes to the fact that he was the Son of God. He came back also that he might tell us the truth about the grave and deliver us who were in bondage through the fear of death.

What is the truth about the grave? Well, it is just a place and an emptied place at that. "He is not here," said the angel about Jesus. "Behold the place where they laid him!" The place! That was all. And that is true of the grave of every Christian in the world. Over every one we can utter these words: "He is not here!" I am not finding fault with the reverence we feel for the places where we lay our dead. The women took their spices to the grave of Jesus, and we take our wreaths and stones and plant the places where our dear ones lie with roses and forget-me-nots. There is something comforting to one's soul in the care with which the graves of our soldiers are tended wherever they are. It is a natural instinct with us, a bit of the holy constraint of love, to pay honor to the very dust of our dead. But let us remember that our dead are not there and that the grave is only the "place" where we laid them.

We have yet to emancipate ourselves from certain mistaken notions about the end, the end that is not an end at all but rather a fresh start. Some of these mistaken notions are embedded in our most familiar hymns. There is a hymn that says,

> Now the laborer's task is o'er; . . .
> Father, in thy gracious keeping,
> Leave we now thy servant sleeping[3]

as if the grave were his bed. The dead are not asleep at all. They are gloriously awake and alive. They are with Christ. Death is not a state; it is an act. Death is but, as one of our hymns says, "a narrow stream," and one step takes us over it. If you use the term "sleep" about it at all, it is not to suggest a long state of unconsciousness, but rather to take away all thoughts of terror from it. We close our eyes on this world only to open them on the world eternal.

Our dead are not "asleep" in the grave. You may go and visit the place where you laid him—but remember it is an empty place. The emptiest place in our city is the cemetery where we have laid our dead.

The Place of Victory

"Behold, the place where they laid him!" It was an empty place! But empty place though it was, there were certain significant things about it if these poor stunned and bewildered women had self-possession enough left in them to be able to notice. From another Gospel (John 20:6-7) we discover this about the empty place: the Lord left behind him the cloths in which Joseph and Nicodemus had wrapped his body. When Peter went in a little while later he beheld the linen cloths lying and the napkin that was upon his head, not lying with the linen cloths but rolled up in a place by itself. The impression that leaves upon my mind is that of an unhurried exit. Jesus had time, so to speak, to fold up his grave-clothes and lay them tidily by. We speak of the conflict of the cross and grave, and we speak rightly. The eternal conflict between good and evil came to a crisis and a climax in the cross and the grave. Out of that conflict Jesus emerged victor. And it was not a bare victory that He won. He won a complete victory. There were no signs of conflict about Joseph's tomb any more than there were in those Civil War cemeteries which I saw some years ago. Jesus had overcome.

---

[3][John Ellerton, "Now the Laborer's Task Is O'er" (1871).]

And what was it Jesus overcame? To begin with he overcame death. He took death and captivity captive.

What that empty grave reveals is the triumph of life over death. Death is not the last word. If it were, what a heartbreaking world this would be. But death, as Paul says, "has been swallowed up in victory." Indeed, Paul waxes very bold when writing to Timothy and declares that Jesus has "abolished" death. "Abolished it?" you say, "but is not death as busy as ever in our midst? Has he not been very busy in this church of ours during these last months? Has he not made great gaps in our family circles?" Yes, all that is true. Death still tramps through our world snatching at this one and that, and leaving multitudes of broken hearts in his train. Still the empire of death is a broken empire, and one day it will be finally destroyed.

Death, like disease, is an alien in this world of ours. It ought not to be here at all. Christ "rebelled" against death as he rebelled against disease. As he overcame disease so also he overcame death. At long last there will be no death at all and life will be supreme and unchallenged. Even though death seems still so busy, for believing people Jesus has already "abolished" it as "death." It has ceased to be "death." The sting of death is sin. What makes death to be death, that coarse, brutal, terrifying thing, is sin, and Christ for all who love him has abolished death in that sense. He has taken sin away and so robbed death of all its terror. He revealed death as just the passageway to the Father's house and the larger life. "O death, where is thy sting? O grave, where is thy victory? Thanks be to God who giveth us the victory through our Lord Jesus Christ." The bonds of death have been broken. The tyranny of death has been shattered. The face of death is toward the Sun of Life. Behold the place where they laid him, but where death's power could not keep him. Behold the place! The empty place! Christ has abolished death and brought life and immortality to light.

Again, that empty grave speaks of Christ's victory over all the embattled powers of evil. Death is only one of the evidences of evil's power. But it was not simply the rescue of the individual from the power and terror of death that Christ brought about when he rose from the dead; rather he smashed the whole empire of evil. "The kings of the earth set themselves, and the rulers take counsel together, against the Lord, and against his anointed, saying, Let us break their bands asunder, and cast away their cords from us" (Psalm 2:2-3). All the vested interests of evil rose up against Jesus. And on Good Friday when Jesus hung on that Cross, it looked as if evil had triumphed. But he that sitteth in the heavens laughed at plotting priests and princes; the Lord had them in derision. He brought all their schemes and plans to naught.

They killed Jesus, it is true. But they could not destroy him. In the morning the grave was empty. "Behold, the place where they laid him!" When I look at that empty place I know that the evil powers of this world have more than met their match. They have been defeated and broken. Christ took captive all the principalities and powers of evil and in that empty grave he triumphed over them. It is the victory of good; it is the victory of God. The vested interest of evil seems still to be tremendously strong. It seems, sometimes, that we are fighting a losing battle. But when we come to Easter morning and find its message we need not fear or lose hope. "Behold the place!" It is an empty place. The critical and decisive battle was fought on the cross and the empty grave declares the triumph of good.

The Bible declares that the kingdoms of this world are to become the kingdoms of our God and of his Christ. It declares that its people are all to be righteous. It declares that the Lord's house is to be established on the top of the mountains and that all nations are to flow into it. It declares that there is to be an abundance of peace till the moon be no more. It declares that in the name of Jesus Christ every knee is to bow. It declares that it is the Lord who reigns. Staggering as these great promises are I believe them everyone when I "behold the place." All the powers of hell could not and cannot keep him in the tomb.

The Present Friend

The angel said to those loyal but shortsighted women, "Behold, the place where they laid him!" "He is not here," they said. Well, then, if he is not here, then where is he?" Everywhere! He was with them for all of their days. If they had him in the tomb all they would have had would have been a sad memory. What did Jesus instead become to them? He became an abiding presence and a living friend. Because he was not there he was with them everywhere. They went through life with singing souls because they went through it in the company of the living Lord. My friends, we need more than memories to carry us through life. We need a presence, a friend, and an almighty helper. And such a one we have in our living Lord. He says, "Lo, I am with you always even to the end of the world."

The Lord is risen! Come, behold the place where they laid him—for it is an empty place!

And Forget Not All His Benefits

Bless the Lord, O my soul, and forget not all his benefits.
(Psalm 103:2 KJV)

Thanksgiving should be an all-through-the-year proposition. It is something much deeper than a feeling. It's like holding a magnifying glass in front of the pleasures of life. Margaret E. Sangster said, "I see Thanksgiving in all of the small, everyday miracles of our existence." That is the right view of Thanksgiving. In other words, she is grateful for all the benefits that come to her.

The psalmist in this text has been reflecting on the events in his life. He has been searching his heart to learn more intimately its secrets. As he inspects the garden of his soul, he finds that the flower called gratitude is not growing in such profusion as he desires. This Psalm expresses his desire to cultivate this grace. He refuses to allow his soul to become dull and listless while surrounded with God's amazing mercies. He refuses to go through life like a blind man blundering through an art gallery, never seeing anything to thrill him or to bring him to his knees in eager thanksgiving. Therefore he arouses himself out of his sluggishness with this urgent appeal "Bless the Lord, O my soul, and forget not all his benefits!"

As Christians we need to arouse ourselves from the unconsciousness of forgetfulness to the realization of God's mercies, expressing to him our gratitude.

What is gratitude? Gratitude is a cultivated attitude of the soul.

It is the memory of the heart.

It is an outward expression of the inner state of the heart.

It is the music of heaven in the soul.

It is one of the fairest and most useful flowers in the garden of the soul.

It is an assemblage of graces—the gathered honey of the choicest flowers.

It is a mirror of the soul, reflecting the image of its several benefits.

It is a bright rainbow in our spiritual atmosphere, displaying the various orders of the ray that calls it into being.

It is like the orange tree dropping its golden fruit upon the earth whence it derives its nutriment.

It is like the verdant willow bending gracefully its bows to kiss the waters that refresh its roots.

It is like a tidal wave returning all its gatherings to the ocean whence it flowed.

It is like a sunbeam sparkling on the waters and then darting by reflection heavenward.

It is like an infant with its joyous countenance smiling back its mother's love.

It is an awakening echo in the heart, responding to the voice of its benefactor.

It is the vibration of the soul's harp strings under the soft touch of God's benevolence.

Did you ever stop to think of the reason why the Psalms have come, like winged angels, down through the centuries, why they make the keynote of grateful piety in every Christian's soul? Why? Because they are so full of gratitude. "Oh, that men would praise the Lord for his goodness, and for his wonderful works to the children of men!" (Psalm 107:8, 15, 21, 31).

A poor Chinese woman had no money with which to pay a hospital for saving the life of her child. Like all Buddhists, she believed in the transmigration of the soul. Expressing her gratitude to the medical missionary she said, "I have been praying that when I die I may become your donkey and carry you about from city to city in your work."

Gratitude Is a Matter of Choice

It is up to you whether you will be thankful or thankless. If you desire to be grateful, you can be. Just like the Psalmist in his urgent plea, we too can cultivate the attitude of gratitude. If we can cultivate the spirit of hatred, malice, ill-will, and ingratitude then we can also cultivate the flower of gratitude. There is no flower of the spirit too lovely or too beautiful for us to grow in our hearts. If we so desire, regardless of the circumstances, we can cultivate this rare flower. Thanksgiving is indeed a fragrant flower. But many of us are so absorbed with our own wants and needs that our prayers have become petitions for personal blessings. "Bless me, O Lord. Bless my family. Bless my church. Bless my country." We don't make it quite as selfish as the old rhyme puts it: "Bless me and my wife, my son John and his wife, us four and no more." Nevertheless, how seldom do any of us get much beyond mere selfish intercessions. The Apostle Paul said, "With thanksgiving let your requests be made known unto God" (Philippians 4:6).

The prayers of the American people today should be chiefly prayers of thanksgiving.

Someone has well said, "The fragrant flower of thanksgiving, which blossoms in the heart of God's people, is the result of a little bud called praise which is firmly affixed to the stem and stalk of Christian faith." Praise is the instinctive outburst of adoring worship that rises from the pure heart of one who knows that God is the giver of every good and perfect gift. The Psalms, which are the music room of the Bible, are filled with songs of praise.

How can we cultivate the spirit of gratitude? It is more than merely saying "Thank you" with the lips, though we ought to say that to both God and people. Yet we may be very poor in real gratitude. Too often our gratitude is mere lip gratitude. If it is to be of any real worth, it must come from the heart.

How can we be grateful? By following the advice of the Psalmist: "Forget not all his benefits." He doesn't ask that we remember them all. It is a modest request. He merely asks us not to forget them all. Perhaps the reason we are so thankless is because we are so thoughtless. No wonder Bunyan, in his great allegory, picked out Forgetful Green as the most dangerous bit of road between the City of Destruction and Mount Zion. Its very greenness is born of the millions of mercies that are buried there with no shaft of gratitude to mark their resting place.

We must cultivate the habit of gratitude. Spurgeon said, "Even the little chick never takes a drink of water without looking up and giving thanks." Carlyle said, "Every man should put himself at zero, and then reckon every degree ascending from that point as an occasion for thanks." Dr. John Henry Jowett said, "No one is going to have anything worth calling a harp in glory who has not already harped music in his own soul." Gratitude is not a minor virtue. It is not one of the elementary virtues that may be left behind as we become more mature. I believe that gratitude is essential to the strength of every virtue and that without it every other branch is starved and lean.

What Is It That the Psalmist Would Have Us Remember?

He doesn't tell us to brood over our enemies, people that we feel have despitefully used us. Nor does he say to brood over the petty injuries, slights, and jealousies. Many people would hear the heartbeat of the Divine in life if they were not so busy listening to life's discords. Instead of plucking a beautiful flower to be worn over the heart they gather the thorns to wear them in their hearts. All the day long they are annoyed with the trifling beats of life. If any kindness ever comes to their heart, they kept it a secret.

The psalmist does not tell us to brood over the success of others and contrast them with our seeming inferiority. We like to think that our neighbor is more successful than we. Once a dog went on a foraging trip. His trip was very successful. Having found a nice juicy piece of beef, he took it in his mouth and started for home. But as he was crossing a lovely, clear stream upon a foot log, he saw the reflection of himself in the water. The other dog had a much larger piece of meat than he. He let go of his and jumped into the water after the piece that belonged to the other dog. The result was that he came home empty-handed with a grudge on life for robbing him of that which he had really robbed himself. Surely the wise man was right when he said, "The eyes of a fool are in the ends of the earth" (Proverbs 17:24). He is so busy looking at the things of others that he despises what is his own.

The psalmist tells us not to think of what we don't have but rather of what we have. We are to remember that the things we possess are the gracious gifts of God to us. We can never realize the preciousness of our gifts until we take time to think upon them instead of being envious of the gifts of others.

The story of the "House with the Golden Windows"[1] is a fine illustration of this truth. There lived a lad in a lovely cottage on the western side of a great mountain that overlooked a beautiful valley. Across the valley was a house that was much more beautiful than his. He ceased to be grateful for his and even despised it because this house across the valley had golden windows. He would look across the valley in the early morning as the rays of the sun shone upon it and resolved that as soon as he was old enough, he would leave home and go to this beautiful house. At last that day came. He made the toilsome journey and arrived late in the afternoon at the spot where he thought the wonderful house stood. But he didn't find it. Instead, he found a house more ordinary than his own. He was sure that he had made a mistake so seeing a little girl playing in the yard he asked her

---

[1][Laura Richards, "The Golden Windows," in *The Golden Windows: A Book of Fables for Young and Old* (Boston: Little, Brown, 1903) and in *The Golden Windows and the Silver Crown: A Book of Fables for Young and Old* (New York: Grosset & Dunlap, 1931).]

if she knew where the house with the golden windows was. "Indeed I do," she replied eagerly. And she pointed to his house across the valley, whose windows at that moment were a blaze of golden glory. For the first time he saw the beauty of what was his own and hurried back to it with a grateful heart. You and I live in a house with golden windows if we only had eyes to see, for our windows are made golden by the shining of the Sun of Righteousness who has risen upon us with healing in his beams.

What Are Some of the Benefits That We Should Remember That Will Beget within Us the Grace of Gratitude?

The psalmist doesn't mention the day-by-day graces that we often regard as commonplace because of their constancy. He doesn't mention the coming of the sunrise, the seasons, the bloom of flowers, the song of the birds, the clasp of the hands, and the love of the home circle. It is in the realization that every good and perfect gift is from above, that in the faith that possesses God we possess all else, that he passes at once to the benefits that have come directly from God's hand.

The psalmist thanks God for the revelation of himself through Moses and through the psalmist's personal experience. It is amazing how fully this man has come to know God in spite of the fact that he lived long centuries before the coming of Jesus, who said, "He that hath seen me hath seen the Father."

The psalmist is thankful for the infinite beauty of God that this revelation has disclosed. How winsome, lovely, and adorable he has found God to be. No wonder he falls upon his knees in spontaneous praise and thanksgiving. God is like a father: "Like as a father pitieth his children, so the Lord pitieth them that fear him." How wonderfully it is expressed by Jesus who told us of a boy that went away from home, from friends, from decency and self-respect, but who could never run away from his father's love. His father was always missing him, always longing for him, and always yearning for his return.

The psalmist shows us the forgiving heart of God: "Who forgiveth all thine iniquities." He does so not in a grudging fashion but abundantly and eagerly. "He is plenteous in mercy." He always does things on a grand scale. When he forgives he does so grandly, forgiving literally all our iniquities and removing them as far from us as the East is from the West.

This also means that he takes us back into his confidence. He trusts us as if we had always been true. He forgets that we ever sinned. "He will forgive their iniquity, and will remember their sin no more." It is the only thing in their world that God forgets. He never forgets the least of his children. He never forgets their efforts to serve him. He remembers with infinite appreciation. He turns his back upon our sins and tells us to do the same. "Go and sin no more."

The psalmist is grateful because he has found the source of unfailing youth: "Thy youth is renewed like the eagle's." Men and women in all ages have hated to grow old. Some actually grow older more quickly by trying to keep from growing old. All of us want to remain young as long as we can. But fight as we may this tabernacle of clay is sure to fall into ruin. No secrets of the beautician, no facial surgery, and no Ponce de Leon Fountain of Youth can prevent it. Winter comes to every one of us as far as the body is concerned but we may have a springtime in our hearts and our minds.

Finally, the psalmist is thankful because he has found one that satisfies his soul. In spite of the world of restlessness and weariness and broken hearts and hopes in which he lives, he sings gratefully, "Who satisfieth thy mouth with good things." What shall it profit a man if he gains the whole world and misses God, the one who alone can satisfy the human heart? What have we lost if we miss the things for which people are scrambling and instead find real satisfaction? In England there is the grave of a man who lived and moved in his community like a rich and rare perfume. His tomb bears this inscription: "Here lies a man who was satisfied with Jesus." If that can be truly said of us, we have true reason to offer thanksgiving.

The story is told of a certain tired minister who on a late Saturday afternoon was trying to finish his Sunday morning sermon. His interruptions had been many and his nerves were on edge from sheer weariness. Then came a knock at the door. He braced himself for another drain upon his energies and said "Come in." The door opened and a little girl looked in. "Daddy, may I come in?" she asked. When consent was given, she bounded across the room, climbed into the tired man's lap and began to caress him in her sweet childish fashion. Then she said, "Daddy I didn't come to ask you for a thing. I just came to climb in your lap and hug your neck and kiss your lips and tell you what a good, kind, sweet daddy you are." And so much warmth slipped into his tired heart that it crowded out all the weariness. God is a Father and his heart too warms at our giving thanks to him. Let's cultivate the spirit of gratitude. Therefore, "Let the redeemed of the Lord say so."

Thy Kingdom Come

Thy kingdom come. Thy will be done in earth, as it is in heaven.
(Matthew 6:10 KJV)

These words suggest a motto for coming days. On the closing Sunday of the year many laypeople wish the minister to preach from a golden text that will serve them as a guiding star throughout the ensuing months. In the midst of change and chaos we all need something high and fixed. In a world that has been at war those who love the Lord should be able to steer by the stars and not by the waves.

As a motto for the New Year, what could prove more fitting than the words of our text? They appear in the Sermon on the Mount. "Thy kingdom come!" What could be simpler or more sublime? When rightly understood, these words give the substance of the Christian religion and life. However, through constant use they have become so familiar that sometimes they seem commonplace. If we are to restore their pristine luster, we must remember what they mean.

As if in response to our unspoken question the Master explains this portion of the Lord's Prayer. "Thy kingdom come" means "Thy will be done in earth, as it is in heaven." The kingdom of God, therefore, points to the realm in which his people do his holy will. Ideally, the petition makes us think of heaven. There everyone does the will of the heavenly Father. That is the kingdom of God in glory. But the Lord's Prayer has to do chiefly with mortals here below. It concerns the way we ought to live here and now: "Thy will be done in our community today, as it is done in the City of God evermore." Such modern diction makes us thank God anew for the simplicity of the Master: "Thy kingdom come. Thy will be done in earth, as it is in heaven."

The words suggest three lines of thought about the kingdom of God in our midst today. The first is the most vital; hence that is where we take our start.

The Kingdom Is Divine

This truth may sound simple. Nevertheless, it sums up all we know about religion and life. The kingdom is divine. It is the kingdom of God. Someone may protest, "The Heavenly Father has given the authority to Christ as our King." That is true, most gloriously true. But surely our Lord has taught us to look on the Kingdom as belonging to God the Father Almighty: "Seek ye first the kingdom of God."

In the phrase "the kingdom of God" the stress falls on the word at the end. God founded the kingdom of old. He watches over it now. He guarantees that it will endure forever. Even in the darkest hour of earth he can depend on a host of his servants to be loyal unto death. At the close of the present age his cause will triumph. "The kingdoms of this world are become the kingdoms of our Lord, and of his Christ." Then the Prince of glory shall reign over the earth he died to redeem. How do we know? "We have Christ's own promise, and that cannot fail."

The coming of God's kingdom depends chiefly on him, not on us. That is why we pray, "Thy kingdom come." He who has begun a good work in the world will not cease until that work is finished. Back of his kingdom on earth stands the wisdom and the power as well as the boundless resources of the Triune God. It makes a vast deal of difference to us mortals that we serve the God who perseveres. Whenever we do his will on earth we fall in line with the loftiest and the noblest movements in all the world. Other causes that once seemed as mighty as Gibraltar have crumbled but the kingdom of God shall endure. Whatever reverses the coming year may bring to the forces of truth and honor, those who keep doing the will of God day after day can rest secure. The kingdom must triumph. Back of it stands Eternal God.

In things temporal as well as spiritual it is good to enjoy a sense of security. It is heartening to know that one's investments for home and loved ones are safe. Throughout the land in the 1930s banks large and small were forced to close their doors. In more recent years failures of that sort have become rare. When such an institution goes on the rocks, the depositors need not suffer loss. Back of every bank in our country stands the government of the United States. Hence there should be a sense of security about such investments. In fact, we accept the guarantee of bank deposits as a matter of course.

Why not employ the same principle in a far loftier realm? Even if our government should some day go down, the Word of our God would endure. The feeling of security about things spiritual depends on the fact that God stands back of his kingdom. As his beloved children we are laying up treasures in heaven by doing his will on earth. We can trust him to safeguard those treasures for time and eternity. In brief, here is the best thing we mortals can know about the kingdom: it belongs to God; it is divine. Such a message comes through Richard C. Trench's poem on the Kingdom of God:

I say to thee, do thou repeat
  To the first man thou mayest meet
In lane, highway, or open street—
  That he and we and all men move
Under a canopy of love,
  As broad as the blue sky above; . . .
Yet, if we all one Guide obey,
  The dreariest path, the darkest way
Shall issue out in heavenly day;
  And we on diverse shores now cast,
Shall meet, our perilous voyage past,
  All in our Father's house at last.[1]

The Kingdom Is Human

The words "Thy kingdom come" mean "Thy will be done in earth." In other words, the kingdom is human. In its source and in its power the Kingdom must ever be as divine as God himself. It is the realm where he lives and moves and has his being. But from our point of view the kingdom must also be human. If it could speak it might exclaim, "Nothing human is foreign to me!" To God's children here below life should prove simple at its heart. Being Christian ought to mean doing the will of our Heavenly Father. Insofar as we mortals can tell, this world is the only part of God's universe where the will of our God is not being done. Is it any wonder then that we mortals pray: "Thy kingdom come"?

The kingdom comes as a rule to one person at a time. Sooner or later every one of us must face the question "Am I living to do the will of God, or am I trying to go my own way?" Surely the best time to become a Christian and to start doing the will of God is in the beauty of life's morning. Would that every growing boy or girl in our community might be a Christian this morning! By a Christian I mean being like Jesus when he was that age and size. Then it would not be long before we should begin to remake our part of the world. That is why Horace Bushnell's classic book,

---

[1][Richard Chenivix Trench, "In Our Father's House at Last," in *Elegiac Poems* (London: E. Moxon, 1843).]

Christian Nurture, contains a chapter on "The Out-Populating Power of the Christian Stock." He means that the ideal way to advance the Kingdom of God on earth is to win the boys and the girls one by one.[2]

If not in childhood, then the time to become a follower of Christ is before one crosses the threshold into manhood or womanhood. Among all the vital choices that confront any youth or maiden the most momentous is this: Whom shall I serve, God or myself? Shall I make it my chief concern to do the will of the Heavenly Father, or shall I insist on having my own way? It is said that when Aaron Burr reached the age of twenty-one he faced this issue squarely. Deliberately he resolved to turn his back on the God of his fathers. Doubtless for this reason one of the most brilliant men in American history made a shipwreck of his life. Today at Princeton Cemetery his bones lie buried at the foot of his grandfather's grave. Those two, Jonathan Edwards and Aaron Burr, illustrate the difference between the man who seeks first the Kingdom of God and the one who chooses slavery to self.

If not in childhood or youth, the time to start doing the will of God is in mature manhood or even old age. Whatever a person's years, the hour to get right with God is the one now ready to strike on the clock. In the scriptures the majority of the conversions recorded took place after youth had fled. Now that hosts of men and women have become disillusioned with the world, after years worse than wasted in chasing phantoms, why should they not turn to God? In making up an inventory at the end of the year, why should the businessman not determine to start out afresh and live henceforth on a Christian basis? "Seek ye first the kingdom of God, and his righteousness; and all these things shall be added unto you."

Since the kingdom of God is human, it has to do with everything that concerns our lives. Largely through men and women who have enlisted for the adventure of doing God's will, his kingdom comes to the home and the church. That is why the two institutions exist, as training schools for the children of God and as object lessons for other folk. What a wholesome and happy place our community would be if all of us here at home would resolve to obey the revealed will of our Lord. In such an ideal community "love is an unerring light, and joy its own security."

----

[2][Horace Bushnell, *Christian Nurture* (New York: Charles Scribner, 1861; 1860).]

What then, is the "will" to which we should look as the summum bonum on earth and in heaven? According to the apostle Paul, foremost interpreter of the Christian faith, the kingdom of God means "righteousness, and peace, and joy in the Holy Spirit" (Romans 14:17). In other words, the will of the Father means the very best that he can devise for us who dwell in a world full of hatred, greed, and strife, a world often cursed by war, and a world with all its by products forged in hell.

During the coming year, or even during this one week, if everyone here at home would start doing the will of God gladly and well, our part of earth would seem like the City of God. If every man or woman, boy or girl, would live as an advance agent of the kingdom, there would be justice between person and person, peace between group and group, and joy between earth and heaven. All this and vastly more we ought to mean whenever we pray: "Thy kingdom come. Thy will be done in our community and to the ends of the earth." In the words of George MacDonald, "The kingdom of heaven is [fully] come . . . when God's will is our will."[3]

Thus far we have looked on the kingdom as divine and human. It is as divine as God and as human as people.

The Kingdom Is Also Practical

It is as practical as everyday living. Sometimes our church talk about the kingdom sounds like "the unilluminating discussion of unreal problems in unintelligible language."[4] Of course none of us can fathom the depths of this truth or reach up far enough to measure its height. According to masters of Christian doctrine, the Kingdom must be both "eschatological and ethical." It has everything to do with the "final things" at the end of this present age. But at present we are concerned with the practical bearing on life in our workday world.

"Thy will be done!" It is not only to be preached and prayed and sung; it is to be done! These four little words in our text show what it means to be a Christian: "Thy will be done!" To become a disciple of the Lord, one needs to accept him as savior and king. When one has taken that step, the

---

[3][George MacDonald, *David Elginbrod* (London: Hurst and Blackett, 1863) pt. 2, "Arnstead"; chap. 12, "A Sunday with Falconer."]

[4][Andrew W. Blackwood, *The Preparation of Sermons* (New York: Abingdon-Cokesbury Press, 1948) 30.]

chief business of life on earth becomes the doing of God's will. The followers of Christ as Lord may differ in heart and life as much as in appearance and ways of speech. But they should all be alike in one respect: everyone should stand loyal to Christ as King. Madame Chiang Kai-shek and Dr. E. Stanley Jones ought to cherish the same sort of loyalty as the humblest person and the unknown soldier of the cross. One and all, the citizens of the kingdom live and strive to do the will of God. "Love seems divine when duty becomes a joy."

Is it any wonder that being a Christian proves hard? In fact, apart from divine grace it is impossible day after day to do the will of God on earth as it is done in heaven. To be a follower of the Nazarene takes all of a person's time, strength, and lifeblood. Much of our God-given energy should go into the advancement of the kingdom through the home and the church. If a person calls someone to serve on the farm, office, or store, or factory, that too is the appointed place for him to seek first the Kingdom of God. Such a message comes from Shakespeare in *Measure for Measure*:

> Heaven doth with us as we with torches do,
> Not light them for themselves; for if our virtues
> Did not go forth of us, 't were all alike
> As if we had them not. Spirits are not finely touch'd
> But to fine issues. . . .   (*Measure for Measure* 1.1.33-37)

This story comes to us from a brother pastor of the Methodist Church. The church of which he was pastor had as their guests on a Sunday night just before New Year's a throng of businesswomen together with their friends. Some of those women were finding it hard to preserve "the white flower of a blameless life." Hence they welcomed the pastor's sermon about "The Religion of a Businesswoman." On the basis that every person's life should be a plan of God, the clergyman declared that a Christian businesswoman, such as Lydia in the Acts of the Apostles, may serve God as well as the minister or the missionary in Africa. The next day the pastor received a letter from a young woman whom he did not know as she belonged to another congregation. Here is a part of what she wrote:

> For me today and throughout the year this office shall be the house of God and the gate of heaven. While still a girl in college I dreamed of becoming a missionary in Africa, like Mary Slessor. But when my father died I had to come home to help support the family. Often I have almost hated this place of business. But since

this is the place the Lord wishes me to serve him during most of my waking hours, I shall strive to do my duty in the office as gladly and well as my dear father is doing God's will in heaven.

Such a letter raises a question that calls for a practical answer. As we have been thinking together about the Kingdom of God—divine, human, and practical—more than one of you must have been whispering within your heart, "How can I be sure about the will of God for me personally? Evidently he has a different plan for each of his children and a new program for each coming day. How can I learn the will of God for me as his child?"

The answer may lie in the prayer "Thy kingdom come." In response to such a petition the Father God is waiting to reveal his will for each of his children. But remember that he always lays down a condition. Our God is practical. He wishes any such prayer to be sincere. If in your heart you long to learn his will, if with all your might you stand ready to do whatever he makes known, then let your mind be at rest. When the time comes to move forward on the path of duty, he will open the way. Meanwhile pray, because everything depends upon him. When the hour arrives for action, work as though it all rests on you. "If any man will do his will, he shall know."

In the spirit of prayer and obedience you can face this new year unafraid. You have never passed this way before and you can never tell what another hour may bring forth. But rest assured that God knows. He cares. He is ready to make all things work together for your good both now and evermore. Since the path of duty will soon lead you away from the doors of the church, why not bow down and commit yourself unto the Lord? "Thy kingdom come. Thy will be done in earth, as it is in heaven."

You remember the words made famous by His Majesty King George VI during a worldwide broadcast on a New Year's Day:

I said to a man who stood at the gate of the year, "Give me a light that I may tread safely into the unknown." And he replied "Go out into the darkness and put your hand into the hand of God. That shall be to you better than light, and safer than a known way."[5]

---

[5][George VI of Great Britain, Christmas Message 1939.]